MINGOOSE AND CHAPEL PORTH

THE STORY OF A CORNISH VALLEY

John Branfield

Mingoose Books

Wheal Coates

Chapel Porth

Footpath to
Wheal Lawrence

WESLEYAN
CHAPEL
1851

Gun shoot

Cuba Downs

Chapel
Villa

Rose Cottage
Ivy Cottage

Footpath
to
Chapel Porth

Briar Cottages

Min

Mingoose Vale

Wayside

Old Inn C

Shasta Cott

Fernbank

Floral Cottage

Mingoose
Villa

By the Way

Tresco
Farm

Wheal
Charlotte
Moor

To Porthtowan

TOWAN CROSS

Victory Inn

Mo

The Beacon

To
gnes

Footpath
to Spain Downs

Mingoose Barns ☐

Mingoose
Farmhouse

Cottage Green

Trenerry Farm

To
Scoll Cottage
and the old station
→
St Agnes and Truro

oose
House

Cottage

Footpath
to
Scoll Lane
To St Agnes
→
and Truro

awke

N
W E
S

MINGOOSE
*A sketchmap of the roads,
footpaths and dwellings*

First published in 2006 by Mingoose Books,
Mingoose Villa, Mingoose, Mount Hawke, Truro, Cornwall TR4 8BX

ISBN 1-872229-41-7

Designed and Typeset by Carol Locke

Printed by Martyn Kimmins Print, Great Western Railway Yard, St. Agnes, Cornwall TR5 0PD

ACKNOWLEDGEMENTS
The illustrations are mostly from the late Bill Morrison's collection of old photographs, with some taken by himself. I am very grateful to his family for permission to include them. Clive Benney lent postcards from his extensive collection and was most generous with his help. Other photographs were taken by JG Ordish (1901 – 1994), Peter Branfield and Jean and Keith Wilson.

For Diggory Jack, born 13 July 2005,
newest inhabitant of Mingoose House

FRONT COVER
Mingoose Cottage from the
paddock of Mingoose House, c1920

Contents

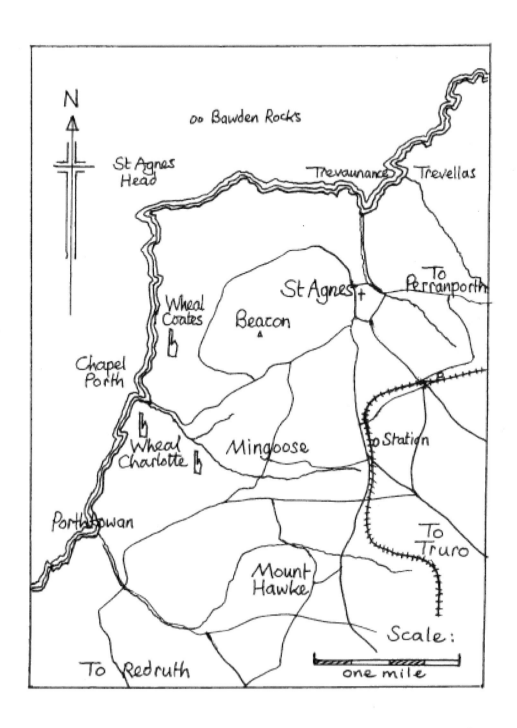

A sketchmap of Mingoose and the surrounding area, near St Agnes in Cornwall

A Cornish Hamlet

CHAPTER ONE

This is not the story of a Cornishman who could not make up his mind. It is the portrait of a hamlet - a village, the old men would have called it - of about twenty households, lying in the valley of Mingoose, a mile to the south of St Agnes Beacon on the north coast of Cornwall. The stream through the valley flows into the sea at Chapel Porth.

It is a quiet, rural sort of place, with woods and a few green fields on the hillsides and heather and gorse at the seaward end. It is hard to imagine that it was once a noisy, industrial complex, a 'beehive' as the old people used to describe it. There were tin and copper mines, with all the engine houses, workshops, stamps and buddles that were associated with them, as well as the shafts and the tips of mine waste. Since they were abandoned in the early part of the last century, the buildings have disappeared apart from the remains of one or two engine houses. Bracken has grown over the paths and tramways, and heather partially covers the spoil. There are few traces of the industrial past.

I have heard about Mingoose as it was from many people, having collected their stories over the years. Edwin Tredinnick was born in Mingoose over a century ago. His great-grandfather lived in Mingoose Cottage and his grandfather and father were born there, though he was born in 'the big house'. Shortly before his death he recorded some memories on tape, with interruptions from his cat purring into the microphone. His earliest memory was of being carried in his father's arms up to the chapel in the Great Blizzard of 1891 and looking across the valley filled with snow.

His daughter Betty was also born in Mingoose, at the bungalow her father built after returning from California. She has written a life of her father from his notes, and her cousin Bill Morrison wrote about the area in his own life story. Although he was born in London, his mother was Eddie's sister and he always spent his childhood holidays with his Cornish grandparents. Later he lived here himself and the cottage is still occupied by the sixth and seventh generation of the same family. My daughter Susan interviewed some of the older residents for a school project in the late sixties, and I have her record of these conversations with May Morrison and Carrie Yelland, Bill's mother and aunt.

I have also drawn upon the memories of Ernest Landry, who made several tapes just before he died. He was born at Nancekuke, on the other side of Porthtowan, but he knew the whole district well and was in the same class as Eddie Tredinnick at Mount Hawke School. Many of the stories I have heard about Mingoose, particularly details of tin-mining in the valley, came from Carrie Yelland's son, Martin. He belonged to a younger generation, but as a boy he must have listened to the stories of the old men and remembered them. He never recorded all the information that he possessed, even though one of his enthusiasms was tape-recording in the days of cumbersome equipment before cassettes. He used to set up loudspeakers on the hillside and play tapes with the volume amplified. Sometimes in winter I would come out of the house and it would sound as though a pack of hounds was coming through the valley. The baying voices echoed from side to side and the noise rooted me to the spot. It was Martin Yelland with one of his tapes. Another was of church bells.

His two great themes were Cornwall and religion. The two came together in his conviction that Jesus had visited Cornwall as a child. Joseph of Arimathea was a tinner and brought him - it is usually said - to the Carnon Valley. But Martin believed that Christ had come to Trevellas, the next valley to the sea beyond Trevaunance on the other side of St Agnes. He had various proofs

The former Miners' Arms
in the nineteen-thirties

8

A horse and covered van come around the corner at the bottom of the valley, c1920

of this - something to do with the Glastonbury thorn - but I usually tried to steer him away from religion and on to Cornish subjects. His great passion here was Richard Trevithick, or Saint Trevithick as he always called him. He believed that there had been an English conspiracy to play down his achievements and to give the credit to George Stephenson. It was Trevithick - Saint Trevithick - who first used steam for locomotive power. If he had been English instead of Cornish, he would have been more honoured and more famous.

Martin had a theory about the meaning of the name Mingoose. I thought it was easy to understand, even for someone with very little Cornish. I took the first part to be men meaning stone, as in menhir, and the second part to be a variation on cos meaning wood. It is familiar in the endings of other place names as cooth, gooth or goose. Mingoose, the stone in the wood. That would not be very surprising, as all the valleys to the north coast were wooded, and many still are. It is one of the contrasts of the area, the sudden descent from bare and open uplands into tree-filled combes. The stone would refer to a standing stone or Celtic cross.

He agreed with the stone, but said that guz is Cornish for blood, and so Mingoose means 'bloodstone'. It was an ancient place of sacrifice, linked with the fire-worshippers of the Beacon. Having said this, he paused and looked sideways through the pebble lens of his glasses. He always wore a bobble hat, pulled well-down over his ears. He waited to see what I made of it. I could imagine the stone in the valley, the sacrificial victim, human or goat, bound to it and hooded figures standing in a circle as they prepared the

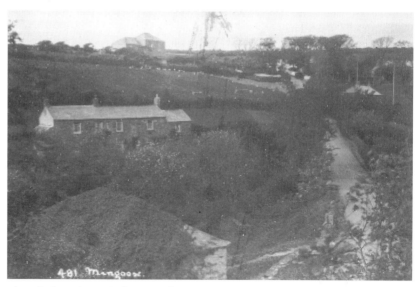

Mingoose Hill, with Briar Cottages and the roof of the old barn, c1920

ritual slaughter. Minguz, the stone of blood.

Martin liked to tease. 'Confuse the buggers' is the motto of the Cornish, according to Charles Causley. Misleading the stranger is a way of preserving your own identity, though Martin half-believed his own inventions. The latest research into place names is unequivocal: myn means edge or border and cos means wood. Mingoose in the end means – less romantically but more interestingly – the edge of the wood. Mankind and wildlife have always been drawn to the edge, the seashore or the side of an estuary, the shelter of trees overlooking open countryside.

When I see old photographs of the area I am struck by the lack of trees, destroyed by the mining industry's need for fuel or for pit props. Today they have been allowed to grow in the hedgerows and several fields have been planted as woods. The name is once more appropriate. Its earliest documented use is in 1317 when it was referred to as Mengoys. In 1327 it was spelt Meyngoys and in 1330 Myngoys. About the time when Cornish was disappearing as the language spoken in the valley, it was written as Mingus Vean in 1516 and Myngoes in 1577. By the next century it had become Mingoose, though as late as 1913 the photographer of the tea-treat was spelling it Mingoes. The need to give it an English sense is strong and we get letters addressed to Mongoose, Minigoose or Mingorse.

I came to the 'edge of the wood' in the census year of 1961, the year in which the population of Cornwall, which had been in decline throughout the twentieth century, began to rise again until it surpassed its nineteenth century peak. I have no family connection with Cornwall, but I was searching for something which I found in Cornwall at large and in Mingoose in particular. Some people find their true home in the place where they were born, others have to seek it out. The valley of Mingoose and Chapel Porth is where I feel most myself. The incomer sometimes has more need to learn all he can about a place than the person to whom it has always been there, taken for granted. I am interested in everything about the area, the way it was and is now, how it has been affected by the passing of time, by continuity and change. It is where Pep and I have brought up our four children, where we have worked or returned home from work. We have known the people who have lived here and heard about those who were here before. I have walked the path through the valley to the sea most days.

It is a microcosm of Cornwall; it represents in miniature the history of the county – or country, as Martin Yelland would have it. In the past the cliffs, moors and valleys were worked for tin and copper. With the collapse of mining at the end of the nineteenth century the men who lived here were forced to emigrate, some like Edwin's father, James Tredinnick, returning to their wives and children and others settling abroad. In the twentieth century the area became popular with holiday visitors. The mining scars on the landscape healed and the stone-built engine houses and chimneys began to be valued as industrial relics. It is now scheduled

A pony and jingle
on Mingoose Hill

The ruined mine buildings
of Wheal Coates

as an Area of Outstanding Natural Beauty and the coastline and
the Beacon are owned by the National Trust. The story of Mingoose
and its people – the Tredinnicks and Yellands, Rickards, Murrishes
and Pascoes, Rashleighs and Retallacks, all names that have
disappeared from the valley – is the story of the whole of Cornwall
over the years.

The Beacon

CHAPTER TWO

As you drive down the A30, you first catch sight of St Agnes Beacon from the hill on the dual carriageway that bypasses Indian Queens and Fraddon. It is still ten or twelve miles away, no more than a low mound in the distance, somewhere out towards the north coast. It reappears again from time to time and after Carland Cross it lies ahead. It begins to take on the familiar shape of a crouching lion, its hindquarters to the sea, its forepaws to the south, its head raised and the tip of its nose formed by the rocks below the brow. Whenever I see it, I feel that I am nearing home and my spirits rise.

You leave the main road at Chiverton roundabout, which when we first came here was a simple crossroads with banks on either side - you took your life in your hands as you drove across - and take the B3277 to St Agnes. The route is so direct along Teagle Straight and past Tywarnhayle Farm that the road must first have been made with the hill as a marker. It would have been trodden by people coming up from the south, and with a clear view of the Beacon they headed towards it, rather than towards the village, which lies on the protected eastern side.

According to legend, the earliest visitors approaching from the other coast were the Phoenicians, who came here to trade for tin. The tin was found on the slopes of the Beacon and did not have to be mined. It was in veins exposed at the surface and in the gravel of the streams. They took it back to the Mediterranean, where it was blended with copper to make bronze for weapons and ornaments. It may only be a legend, but the area was certainly worked for metals from the earliest times and it was an important source of tin for the Romans. A golden coin of Valentinian was once ploughed up in one of the fields on the slopes.

The track to the Beacon may also have been made by people going there to worship. Martin Yelland had a theory about it. The village used to be known, he said, as St Ann or St Annes. This is confirmed by old maps of Cornwall. All the seventeenth century maps, with one exception and with various spellings, give the name as St Annes. On eighteenth century maps it becomes St Agnes.

The view of the Beacon and Mingoose
Chapel from the Porthtowan road

THE BEACON

According to Martin, St Ann was a substitution for an earlier Celtic name and the version that he favoured - this is where it becomes a bit fanciful - was Santan. The Cornish san or sans means 'holy', and tan means 'fire'. Holy fire. The name was pagan; it recalled the use of the Beacon by sun-worshippers, who lit ritual bonfires at the summer and winter solstices.

But even though it had been Christianised into St Ann, it still sounded Cornish, and ordinary people would have heard in the name its original meaning. There was every reason for the English clergy to promote the name of St Agnes. She was a popular saint, a symbol of innocence and purity represented by the lamb or agnus. She disguised the Celtic origins of the place.

The church was dedicated to St Agnes as early as the fourteenth century, but it took three or four hundred years for the spelling to be changed, and even then the parishioners stubbornly clung to the old form. A guide book of the nineteenth century states that 'St Agnes is pronounced by the inhabitants with the g silent to distinguish it from St Agnes, one of the Scilly Isles'. This is unlikely; they would never have had any need to differentiate between the two places. They kept the name St Annes because that was their version (though even that was already second-hand) and they were not going to have it taken from them. It survived amongst some of the older people until recent times, though I have only heard it used self-consciously.

Another old name for the district was Bryanack, which possibly means a high-peaked hill (the Beacon). The name 'Ann' could just as well - though less interestingly - have come from

14

this. It is now generally thought to come from stenes, meaning 'place of tin'. But the process of change that Martin described is probably true: it is a process of colonisation, of Christian ritual taking over from pagan, of English meaning taking over from Cornish.

The Beacon from Spain Downs

The Beacon continues to be associated with fire. In recent years there have been midsummer bonfires; others were lit in celebration of the end of the First World War and the relief of Mafeking. Before that it was one of a chain of bonfires intended to spread the news of invasion by the French at the time of the Napoleonic war, when two soldiers were stationed there and when it had a tower on top, a Gothic folly or summer-house known as Donnithorne's or Unwin's Castle.

From the Beacon the land slopes down to St Agnes Head, high above the sea. The mass of harder rock, the granite thrusting through the slate, survives in the height of the Beacon and the thrust of the headland into the sea. It re-occurs offshore in two islands, known as Bawden Rocks (or Man and his Man, or Man and his Dog, or Cow and Calf). The landscape is predominantly brown heath, with rectangles of green where the fields protrude into the moorland. In early summer the cliffs are yellow with gorse. Later, the heather shows through the blond grass on the moor, rising up the sides of the Beacon like a slow-burning fire.

There are clay pits on this seaward slope, where the miners dug the clay with which they stuck the candles to their hats. Beneath the layer of clay there is a beach, with pebbles and sand, high up on the sides of the Beacon. To the miners this was evidence of the extent of the Flood in the time of Noah. Today, some of the clay is used for pottery and the sand is quarried.

The mine buildings of Wheal Coates stand on top of the cliffs, an engine house which has lost its chimney, some walls and roofless sheds, and a stack rising straight out of the ground. It was where Eddie Tredinnick's father, James, worked as a miner in the 1870s. The ruins have been preserved by the National Trust and in their own austere way are as dramatic as those of a Greek temple standing out against the sea. Lower down the cliff, perched on a ledge above a sheer drop, is the engine house of Towanroath shaft. There used to be a plaque on the side, above the grating over the shaft, which said: 'This engine house was built in 1872 to house the pumping engine which kept the mine-workings free of water. The mine closed about 1885 and the engine, which had a cylinder 36" in diameter, was then dismantled. The building was no longer safe, and was repaired by the National Trust in 1973.' It is one of the best-known images of Cornwall, appearing on the jacket of Daphne du Maurier's Vanishing Cornwall (printed in reverse in early editions).

Beyond the chimney and walls on the cliff face are the bays of Chapel Porth and Porthtowan. If the tide is out, far below is a stretch of sand with the Atlantic waves breaking on the shore. In summer - and often in winter too - the water is greenish-blue, with different shades of blue towards the horizon and with the purple shadows of clouds. White skeins of foam stretch between the breakers, and other lines of foam mark the current sweeping up the coast and around St Agnes Head.

Further west is the collapsed arch of the Tobbin Rock and Gull Island off Portreath. The long line of the North Cliffs stretches unbroken towards Godrevy Island. If the sun is shining, the lighthouse - the lighthouse of Virginia Woolf's To the Lighthouse, although she transposed it to the Western Hebrides - shows up white; at night it flashes once every five seconds. Behind Godrevy lies St Ives, sometimes a misty blur in the distance, sometimes so clear that the sun reflects from individual windows and car roofs.

From the top of the Beacon the other high points of the south-west peninsula are visible. Behind St Ives is Trencrom and nearer lies the ridge of Carn Brea, with the Castle and the Basset memorial, a column like a dumpy candlestick erected by 'grateful' miners to the mine-owner Lord Basset. Each hill-top had its giant, and the one who lived on the Beacon was Giant Bolster. He was the rival of the giant who lived on Carn Brea and the sides of Carn Brea ('stony hill') are littered with boulders which come from St Agnes, thrown there by Giant Bolster in his battles against his enemy. In another version, Giant Bolster could stand with one foot on the Beacon and the other on Carn Brea. If giants are a folk memory of powerful tribal chiefs, then one story illustrates the rivalry between two neighbouring lords, the other the conquest of Carn Brea by the St Agnes clan.

Giant Bolster terrorised the district and it was St Agnes - the saint, not the village - who defeated him. He changed his wife

Carnsight below the Beacon

every year and one year he fell in love with St Agnes. He pestered her with his unwelcome attentions and made her life unbearable, until at last she decided to get rid of him. She said that she wanted one more proof of his love. If the giant would fill a small hole in the cliff at Chapel Porth with his blood, she would know that his love was true. The giant cut his arm and let the blood flow into the hole on the cliff. But he didn't realise that it was a mine shaft with an adit that drained into a cave. His blood flowed into the sea. The stain is still there on the cliff face.

"Is it really?" asked Susan and Frances, aghast, when I pointed out the red mineral-stained rocks.

"Well, that's the story," I said, taken aback by their conviction.

It is a story which is now re-enacted every year on Bolster Day, when the figure of the giant, manipulated by long poles, appears dramatically over the hillside at Chapel Porth.

Early guide books say that the Beacon is a magnificent viewpoint, with 'panoramic vistas' to St Ives, fifteen miles to the south-west and to Trevose Head, seventeen miles to the north-east. On a clear day you are supposed to be able to see thirty - some say thirty-four - churches, though I have never counted them. You are also supposed to be able to look right across the peninsula and see ships at anchor off Falmouth and the top of St Michael's Mount, which seems unlikely. It is possible, though, to make out the shape of Nare Head, some sixteen miles away on the other coast.

To the south of the Beacon, the land appears to form a level tree-less plain between St Agnes and Carn Brea. But the flatness of the plain is deceptive, for it is scored by several deep and narrow valleys. They are formed by streams which flow west and then turn north, to enter the sea where the high cliffs are broken by the coves of Chapel Porth, Porthtowan and Portreath.

The first of these valleys is right at the foot of the Beacon. The stream flowing through Wheal Lawrence valley into Chapel Coombe cuts off the Beacon to the south and west. There is another deep valley to the east, formed by the stream running down to Trevaunance beach. Only a neck of higher ground, which the road into the village follows, separates the two. Apart from this, the Beacon is surrounded by a natural moat. And at some time the work of fortifying the Beacon was completed by digging a dyke which linked Chapel Coombe to Trevaunance. It was described by Richard Carew in The Survey of Cornwall (1602) as a 'fosse', varying in height from six to twenty feet, while it was twenty feet wide in places. It can still be seen. The most complete section is on the Chapel Porth road out of St Agnes near Bolster Farm.

Wheal Lawrence valley was extensively mined and silver was probably found amongst its minerals. Its name would come from Wheal Awrence, the Cornish for Silver Mine, and the elision of the 'l' transformed it into English. The north-facing side is mostly mine waste, steep tips of bare screed. The south-facing slope is warm and luxuriant. Lots of trees grow here: eucalyptus and holly bushes, bamboo and pittosporum, rhododendrons, camellias and azaleas. A swampy patch is filled with gunnera, a sort of giant rhubarb. In winter it resembles a sailing ships' graveyard, the stalks like broken spars and the leaves like the tattered remains of canvas sails. Nearby is a well, a spout in a mossy stone wall with a basin beneath, shaded by overhanging ferns and ivy.

There is a second valley to the south of the Beacon, about a mile away. It runs parallel to the partially artificial valley of Wheal Lawrence and then turns north-west; the two join together to form Chapel Coombe. ('Combe' is usually spelt with two 'o's in Cornwall.) In this valley lies Mingoose.

Scoll Lane

CHAPTER THREE

The stream which runs through Mingoose to Chapel Porth rises near the site of the old railway bridge, where the line from Truro to Chacewater, St Agnes, Perranporth and Newquay crossed the road from Chiverton. The station was a short distance beyond the bridge, a mile from the village. The line was closed in the railway cuts of the sixties and the bridge demolished.

This is the start of the valley, just a gentle dip in the land at this point. A lane leaves the road, dropping down the slope to follow the beginnings of the stream. It winds into the landscape, gleaming in wet weather like a road in an old woodcut. On the corner stands Scoll Cottage. It was once a dame school, where the pupils paid a penny a week for their education; sometimes in mining areas like this they paid in candles. It was a farm labourer's cottage, tied to Mingoose Farm and its earlier use seems to have given the lane its name, but behind that lies an even earlier meaning from the Cornish for hazel trees. These layers of meaning, lying like shadows one beneath the other, give a poetic quality to the names of places. They can be fluid and at different times and in different families it has been known as Mingoose Lane and Station Lane. The cottage stood empty for some years; its windows were smashed and boarded up, and there was barbed wire across the gates. Then it was restored and enlarged.

After a while, the lane leaves the stream and keeps higher up along the side of the valley. It is very narrow, between stone banks, and if two cars meet, one of them has to back, though very little traffic comes this way. In summer the grasses on the banks, sorrel and campions and foxgloves grow inwards and brush both sides of the car as it passes through. The late afternoon sun dazzles the driver. A strip of green weeds, the ones that smell of pineapple when they are crushed, grows in the middle of the road.

On the right is the entrance to a farm, a sloping triangle of grass with an apple tree in the centre, and a drive between banks and pine trees up to the house. It has bluebells along it in the late spring. The farmhouse stands on top of the slope, a severe Georgian building with barns around it and trees on the side away from the sea.

A train leaves St Agnes Station and approaches the bridge at the head of the Mingoose Valley, c1910

Scoll Cottage before renovation

Mingoose Farm, c1980

After an S bend in the road, two sharp right-angles to get around more farm buildings, comes the narrowest part of the lane. There is a sense of being high up, of being not far from the coast. Nothing grows on top of the banks or hedges. This opens out to a small patch of turf which has now been fenced. It looks across to the other side of the valley, which has not been visible so far because of the high banks. This patch of land was known as Mingoose Green, the site of an annual feast-day fair. It is still known in our family as the Green, and a quick walk up to the Green was as far as the dog went on a wet winter's evening. No one else calls it the Green; I heard the name from Martin Yelland.

It is a place we needed a name for, but it does strike me as unlikely. It sounds like the deliberate re-creation of a village life that is long past, with its associations of cricket under the elm trees and sitting outside at a country pub. It is not that sort of green and there is hardly a tree in sight. It is difficult to imagine a fair taking place on such a tiny patch. What sort of stalls were there? Who patronised them? It must have been a very small concern, a few booths and perhaps some farm animals for sale. When I have mentioned it to anyone else, it has always drawn a blank. Eddie Tredinnick had never heard of it. I began to wonder if Martin had made it up, but then I found a reference to an estate map of 1813. Amongst all the field names of Mingoose Farm - Oppy's Meadow, Higher Trahan, Park Dray, Lamb Park, Little Gwins and Park Onion - appears Mingoose Green.

Just past the Green is a cottage that was derelict for years. All the front had collapsed, half the roof and one end-wall. Ivy climbed over the chimney. There were a lot of houses in Mingoose which have simply vanished. It had a much greater population at one time, when the mines were working in the valley and there were enough inhabitants to fill a chapel or patronise a fair. Eddie Tredinnick could count up to twenty houses that disappeared in the valley in his lifetime. The Gazetteer of Cornwall of 1884 recorded about fifty 'tenements' in Mingoose; today there are about half that number.

Most of the cottages were built of cob, or clob as it is called locally, and once the roof had gone - and many were roofed with straw, there is still one thatched cottage in Mingoose - the rain soon soaked into the clay and the cottage melted back into the

The derelict cottage in Scoll Lane

ground. All that remains are a few stones and a mound of earth, some garden flowers growing nearby and the blossom of an apple tree in the spring. If they were made of stone, they were pillaged for building materials and the stones incorporated into new buildings or hedges. This was often the fate of engine houses when they were no longer in use.

An abandoned cottage in
Wheal Lawrence, later rebuilt

The cottage in Scoll Lane was still lived in when we first came here. Earlier the Whitfords brought up five daughters in this small space, Violet, Priscilla, Ethel, Dora and Clarice. When Eddie Tredinnick was a boy, Jemima Bartle lived there. Her husband was known as 'Happy' Isaac and he bred rabbits; Ernie Landry liked to go and see them. It had once been the home of Eddie's great-grandfather, a James Tredinnick who was a carrier. Betty knew her great-aunt Fanny who remembered as a girl going to feed her grandfather's horses. This would have been in the 1850s, a century and a half spanned in one conversation.

After it was condemned, the cottage was bought by a man from London, who used to visit from time to time and had a caravan in the front garden. Then the caravan disappeared. Its condition deteriorated, but it still looked as though it could be renovated. In the summer, visiting cards were sometimes pinned to the doorpost: 'If you are interested in selling this property, please phone this number.' During a winter storm the end wall collapsed and holes appeared in the roof. Part of it was covered with corrugated sheets and some of these were blown away. A barn owl lived there for a while. The garden filled with brambles. No one left notes on the door jamb any more.

Towards the end of the century the plot was sold and planning permission sought to rebuild the cottage. It was refused at every level until it went to the High Court in London where a judge ruled that a house was preferable to a ruin. I was dismayed at the time, but it was rebuilt with local stone and fits in well. When Mingoose Farm was sold it was split into three, the farmhouse, the land to the south of the lane with a barn conversion to create Trenerry Farm, and the barns with all the land to the north to become the new Mingoose Farm. Then the barns were sold separately and a long dispute began with planning over a new farmhouse. It was eventually built away from the lane towards Spain Downs. This is how new buildings appear in the countryside, although it is supposed to be protected from development.

I think of the farm as it was when Rex Williams or his sister Peggy would bring their herd of South Devons in for milking. Often going home in the car from the school where I taught in Camborne I would meet them in the lane. I switch off the engine. The cows approach suspiciously. The leaders stop in front of the bonnet and stare, but the pressure from the herd behind pushes them on. They divide and flow around the car, a sea of thick brown hides. They keep coming, slow and heavy. Some go by without seeing the car, others check for a moment before being pushed on. One thrusts her face against the window. A tail swishes against the glass.

A cow that hasn't seen the car suddenly stumbles into it. There's a moment of panic, her head lifts, her eyes show white. With no room to go back, and none on either side, it seems as though she might rear up and plunge on to the bonnet. But she pushes against another cow and brushes down the side of the car, which sways and lurches. There are about fifty of them to go by. I feel their great weight, the mass of the whole herd. The car is like an eggshell in their midst. If a few of them leaned against it, it would crumple and give way. They go solidly past, their breath hanging about them. Rex and Peggy bring the herd in calmly, without any drama.

When I drive on, there are fresh cowpats on the road and I hear the tyres squelch through them. The cars in Mingoose at that time were always splashed with dung, freckled patterns which fanned out from the front wheels over the sides and windows. In summer the cowpats dried in the sun and as they shrivelled and curled, they lifted the tarmac from the road.

At the end of Scoll Lane is a junction with a triangle of grass in the centre. The road to the right leads to St Agnes and Chapel Porth, to the left it drops down steeply into Mingoose. At one time this area was referred to as 'Covent Garden'. There was a Vegetables for sale sign on Mr Martin's gate and he lived in a caravan in the field below. Mr and Mrs Trerise also sold vegetables from their house opposite the end of the lane, next door to the Wesleyan chapel of 1851. A track leads out to the gun shoot on Cuba Downs.

Jean Trerise selling vegetables, c1980

The Road Through the Valley

CHAPTER FOUR

The other approach to Mingoose is from the west. The coastal road from Porthtowan comes up the steep hill out of that valley and continues past Wheal Towan, one of the richest copper-mining districts in Cornwall, where Thomas 'Guinea-a-minute' Daniell made the fortune that enabled his son Ralph to buy Trelissick in 1805.

On our first visit to Cornwall we parked here, in a lay-by at the side of Wheal Charlotte moor. We had Stephen with us in our Austin van, but had left Susan and Frances with their grandparents in Devon. We looked across to the Beacon, and considered the places we had seen and where we might live. We liked the Penwith area, it seemed to be the 'real' Cornwall. We fancied a house near St Ives.

We drove on past the Victory Inn, noticing the green sign of Devenish Brewery but not seeing right opposite the pub an unsignposted lane dropping into a valley. I don't know if Mingoose has any official limits. The Ordnance Survey shows a wood, Mingoose Plantation, way back along Teagle Straight, well outside my mental map of the place. For me, it is the valley towards the sea at Chapel Porth and is bounded by the chapel to the north, Scoll Cottage to the east and the Victory Inn to the south-west. It is part of the parish of St Agnes; our children used to go to school there, though earlier generations went to Mount Hawke. The postal address is Mount Hawke, the telephone exchange is Porthtowan. When we tell anyone how to find us, we always say, "Don't go anywhere near Mount Hawke. The landmark is the Victory Inn."

Opposite the inn lies Wheal Charlotte moor, with the Beacon just showing above low heather and gorse. The lane descends transversely across the hill with a field on either side and hedges full of stonecrop and polypody. There is a road narrows sign in a hawthorn bush and the edge of the sign has been flicked back by a passing lorry. The first house on the left is Tresco Farm, with a stone barn against the road. A little further on is Somerville, one of two bungalows built in Mingoose in the twenties and thirties. The lane drops steeply at this point. If it is a hard winter and the roads

are icy, this is where the car wheels spin. Drivers were regularly stuck in the pit of the valley, unable to get out one side or the other, but now the winters are milder.

The lane becomes less steep. Elm Cottage, which reverted to its old name of By The Way, stands on the bank, and the long white front of Floral Cottage is below the road on the other side. Beyond a stone wall the road turns beneath trees and the sloping bank of a field. The top of the Beacon disappears beneath the hill and the valley opens up. The sea is like a wall across the end, surprisingly high. The bottom of the V is usually white with breakers. The other side of the valley is bare moorland.

A stone house stands behind low trees, but anyone passing needs to watch the road instead of looking at the house, because the lane turns a blind corner and is only wide enough for one car at a time. The house is called Mingoose Villa, but it has no name on the gate; it is where we live. The road levels out, passing beneath the end wall of the house and through a tunnel of trees. Beyond the house a track branches off to Mingoose Vale and the sea. The road, usually blotchy with patches of shade or damp, continues on a ledge above the garden of Wayside and beneath the high, tree-covered slopes of Fernbank, the bungalow built by Edwin Tredinnick in 1924 on the site of an old cottage that had also been a dame school and which his aunt Frances attended in the 1850s.

When Eddie wanted to buy the derelict building he went to Coulterville in St Agnes, later the Cleaderscroft Hotel, to see Coulter Hancock. Hancock was the steward to many mines and

Tresco Farm, c1980

24

Floral Cottage early in the twentieth century, when it was thatched and divided into two dwellings

estates, a self-made man who owned much of St Agnes including the Beacon. He could ruin anyone who crossed him and many of the farmers feared him. (His family established a firm of Truro solicitors and today our son Stephen is a partner in Hancock Caffin, though there is no longer any connection with the family.) Hancock asked Eddie his name and discovered that he was James Tredinnick's son. "Your father has said some harsh things about me in his time," he said grimly, "and you'll have to pay for them!" But they were able to agree a price and the bungalow was built on the steep slope above the road. When his daughter Betty was about eighteen months old she wandered through the gate that had been left open and fell twenty feet down the bank, landing by the side of a shell-shocked First World War soldier who was convalescing in a nearby cottage. He picked her up and returned her to her distraught mother.

It must have taken thousands of tons of stone to build all the hedges and banks around Mingoose. The men who built them, probably working round about the year 1800, were skilled in their craft. They used 'underground' stones, waste material from the mines. They laid them with the narrow end outwards like books on a shelf and packed them with earth, finishing the hedge with a layer of turf. The plants grew and bound the bank together. They border the roads of Mingoose and the fields, the footpaths and the drainage channels. They have lasted two hundred years - except where wide farm machinery has dragged them out - and if I have

The former inn before the building of Fernbank in 1924

MINGOOSE NR. ST. AGNES.

to repair a stretch, I realise how skilful the 'old men' were. I can never replace all the stones and it never looks the same. I once built a hedge and showed it to Mr Retallack, the blind retired farmer who lived in Shasta Cottage. "That's a nice bit of hedging," he said, passing his hands over it. He thought about it for a moment, and then added, "For a schoolmaster."

Martin Yelland knew all the stones. He would point them out, the ones that had tin in them. They have nearly all been taken now, leaving gaps in the hedges. There were people around with an eye for a good mineral specimen.

At the bottom of the valley, the road turns and passes over a bridge; in the early nineteenth century the stream was crossed by a ford. Close to the stream was The Miners' Arms, now divided into Old Inn Cottage and Shasta Cottage. This was named after Mount Shasta in California by a miner who emigrated and made enough money to return home, buy a cottage and retire. He would stand at his door, pocket watch in his hand, and time the miners who were going to work.

On the other side of the road is Wayside, converted from a barn. Eddie Tredinnick used it as a store for his materials when he was building Fernbank with its steep access. A year or two later it was still a barn and occupied by an eccentric elderly lady who dressed in the height of Victorian fashion with feather boas and heavy jewellery. She lived on the top floor of the barn, accessed

Old Inn Cottage soon after the building of Fernbank

from the road, and her only furniture was a chaise-longue covered with rugs. She kept chickens on the floor beneath and when she was told that she needed to feed them grit she took out her boxes of fine china and started smashing the crockery to smithereens to feed to the hens. Young Betty joined in with a will, until her father came to see what was happening. The old lady had a dandy, a child's cart that she would drag to the top of Mingoose Hill. Tucking in her long skirts, she would ride down at full speed. One day she asked Eddie to mend it as the wheels wouldn't go round. She claimed that someone had put salt on them. Eventually she was taken away by her family and the barn was used for a time as a riding stables. It was made into a house after the Second World War, one of the earliest barn conversions.

From here the road mounts straight up Mingoose Hill, not at an angle to reduce the gradient as it does on the other side of the valley. It passes Briar Cottages on the left, converted from a terrace of three miners' cottages, with an orchard behind a high stone wall, and Mingoose Cottage on the right, the family home of the Tredinnicks. There is a nursery on one side, a field on the other, and then comes Mingoose House, set back from the road and at right angles to it. It has an arched chapel-like window in the end wall and some outbuildings that Mr Retallack called 'the killing house'. When his mother was a girl, she used to come here once a week to help her cousin, butcher Tredinnick's daughter. The two

Mingoose House in the
nineteen-twenties

girls would take a donkey cart down to Trevaunance Quay to sell
meat to the sailors, who bought large amounts to last a voyage.

Mingoose House dates from the fifteenth century, though
most of it is eighteenth century with nineteenth century
modifications. The tithe apportionment of 1841 shows the occupier
as Anthony Williams, who also rented Parc Nor Farm on the road
to St Agnes, Wheal Towan Farm above Porthtowan and several
other properties belonging to the Enys estate. This must be the
Squire Williams that May Morrison talked about to Susan for her
school project. She said he was a bachelor, a member of the
Williams family of Scorrier House. He had the best orchard for
miles around and there were two fish ponds in the garden with a
summer house between them. When he entertained he offered his
guests wine or sherry kept in a recess in the hall. I pictured him as
a sort of Farmer Boldwood in Thomas Hardy's Far From the
Madding Crowd. In fact, the 1851 census shows that he was forty
years old, had a wife Ann and an eight-year-old daughter of the
same name. They had a live-in maid called Mary Letcher.

In the Poldark novels of Winston Graham there are six big
houses - or 'six inhabited by gentlefolk' - and Mingoose House is
the oldest of them, owned by the Treneglos family. This is pure
fiction, the name chosen for its Cornish sound. But the real
Mingoose House had been more substantial in the days of Squire

28

Williams. At some point in the nineteenth century it was reduced in size. There had been a wide double-door entrance under a long granite lintel at the front. This would have opened into a hall with stairs to the first floor and a large open fireplace in the end wall. The doorway was reduced to half its width and a narrow passageway formed. An extra room was created with partition walls, and a cramped staircase fitted in at the back.

It was more suited to the needs of a tenant farmer with a large family. It even had a family-sized privy across the front lawn and beyond the barn. It was a 'three-holer', two holes for the grown-ups and a smaller one at the end with a child's game on the underside of the lid. It remained in use until after the Second World War.

The house was occupied by the Tredinnicks from 1883 to 1921, and they are more associated with Mingoose than any other family, throughout the nineteenth and twentieth centuries. It was here that Edwin Tredinnick was born in 1889. His father James, like so many other Cornish miners, had sought work abroad during the recession in mining in the eighteen-seventies. He left his wife Emily and their two children, Winnie and Herbert, with his mother at Mingoose Cottage. The cottage was enlarged in 1876 when his father had died. His widowed mother needed to provide herself with an income and extended the building to the road, opening a general store on the ground floor. She was helped by her daughter Fanny and daughter-in-law Emily.

James crossed the Atlantic from Liverpool to New York and then travelled by train across the prairies, where vast herds of buffalo still roamed. His journey continued through the foothills of the Rockies, through canyons and deserts and across the Sierra Nevada to Sacramento. In California he mined for gold. A story he told of these days was how a friend, who had to go away for a while, asked him to help hide and bury his gold. James refused, saying that if it was stolen his friend would always suspect him; he preferred not to risk his friendship. James too must have found gold, for on his return he was able to move his family into Mingoose House. Seven more children were born, two boys dying in infancy.

Edwin grew up in a household of women. His eldest sister Winnie came home to live with her parents, repeating the pattern of a generation earlier, when her husband Edward Rickard went to find work in the mines of South Africa. She brought with her four

Bessie and Emily, c1900, daughters of James and Emily Tredinnick

Eddie Tredinnick in front of
Mingoose House soon after the
end of the First World War

daughters, Theresa, Blanche, Addie and Emmie, and they now joined the Tredinnick girls, Bessie, Emily, Carrie and Fanny May. The girls shared the big bedroom with its large half-tester bed. When the noise from the room became too much, Emily would rush in, rather like the old woman who lived in a shoe, and quell them by beating indiscriminately with her slipper any forms beneath the bedclothes.

In South Africa Edward Rickard worked double shifts in order to provide for his family. The effort exhausted him, he fell ill and died. His daughters stayed on in Mingoose House until Winnie remarried. Washdays were long remembered, with the lines of feminine clothing for all ages hung out to dry.

James and Emily slept in a smaller front bedroom and the two boys who remained at home, Martin and Edwin, shared the room above the kitchen. A cherry tree grew outside the window and Eddie remembered leaning out to pick the fruit. Beneath the tree was the well that provided the house with water and because he was small as a child he was always chosen to descend in a bucket to clean the sides, a task he detested. At least he was not sent up the chimneys.

After the Tredinnicks the house was rented by the Weymouth-Wilsons. Wilson acquired his double-barrelled name during the First World War when he was called up for military service. There were several Wilsons amongst the new recruits and so the sergeant distinguished them by prefixing the name of the town they came from. Weymouth Wilson liked the sound of it so much that he kept it after the war and added the hyphen. It did not impress the Cornish, however, and he was known locally as 'Widemouth' Wilson. He left Mingoose House after a very short stay, doing a midnight flit and taking as much as he could with him, even some of the doors. The place was 'open to the wide', as Eddie said.

The Pascoe family were the next tenants, buying the freehold from the Enys estate in 1961. The land was sold separately, but the house retained the garden, paddock and orchard. I always assumed that this orchard in the bottom of the valley alongside the stream was where Squire Williams grew his famous apples. It contained some old Cornish varieties such as Tommy Knights and Eddie said there used to be two sorts called Qualantines and Sops in Wine. But the 1841 tithe map shows the orchard at the side of the house above the paddock, where the Tredinnick children had their pets' cemetery. Eddie was always the preacher at the burial service.

Evelyn and Jean Pascoe lived for over sixty years in the house where they were born, and their brother Jack owned nearby Ivy Cottage. Another brother George was an RAF sergeant who was shot down and killed on a bombing mission over France in 1943. When Evelyn became unwell they decided to move to St Agnes and sold the house to our son Stephen in 1995. Soon after moving in, Stephen had the walls damp-proofed and re-plastered downstairs. The builders found the wide fireplace across the end wall and in the sitting room an arched recess that had been blocked up. It must have been where Squire Williams kept the sherry for his visitors.

Mingoose House in the snow

Ivy Cottage had been tied to Mingoose House in the past and May Morrison – the Fanny May who grew up there – remembered as a girl collecting the rent from the three cottages that were leased with the house. It had been thatched in the nineteenth century, but the only thatched building now in Mingoose is Rose Cottage, standing just behind it. This was where Martin Yelland lived with his mother, Carrie. He always thought the name was too English and tried hard to get people to call it Boscothwyn, but 'the old white house' never caught on. In the nineteenth century the Murrishes lived there. They had a large family, who were friends with the Tredinnick children. They were all free to play in the large sitting room at Mingoose House, which must have been filled with young Tredinnicks, Rickards and Murrishes. James and Emily sought peace in the small parlour. One Christmas James came out to investigate all the banging and found that the boys were playing at 'miners'. They had tunnelled into the passageway wall.

Bobby and Russell Fowler at Vincent's ice cream cart on Mingoose Hill in 1933

Victorian visitors to Cornwall often commented on the indulgence of the Cornish to the young, that children were not taught to know their place. They 'lorded it over their parents' a Midlands schoolmaster complained when he took a post in a West Cornwall village. But to me James and Emily Tredinnick seem heroic; they were loving - if long-suffering - parents.

Beyond Rose Cottage and at the top of the hill are the chapel and the junction with Scoll Lane. When we first came here very little traffic passed through Mingoose. Only two or three households had cars, whereas now every house has at least one. The milkman,

Rose Cottage in the
nineteen eighties

Alan Green from Trenethick Farm, came through the lane daily and a butcher and a baker called twice a week. Raphael Thomas used to deliver vegetables every Saturday evening. He had a horse and a flat-top cart, with a dog tied to the back axle. The vegetables on the cart were covered with a tarpaulin and he had a hurricane lamp to see by. As the horse got older he would arrive later and later, until it was after midnight before he reached Mingoose. Customers left shopping bags for him, with a list and the money hanging on the door. Eventually the horse dropped dead between the shafts.

Jack Rashleigh had a pony and trap. He kept a few cows at Mingoose Vale and every morning he would take a churn of milk up to the Victory Inn to be collected by the milk lorry. Our children used to like the ride, until one morning a wheel fell off on the corner by our house. What for centuries had been the usual means of transport in the valley had come to an end, almost unnoticed and unrecorded.

A knife-sharpener used to call once a year, riding down the lane on his bicycle. When he had any knives or scissors to sharpen, he would jack up his bike and sit on the saddle, pedalling away to turn the grindstone. There was also a chair-mender who carried bundles of sea grass strapped to the crossbar of his bike. He would mend the seats and backs of chairs as he sat cross-legged in the road outside a cottage. The Johnny Onion-men came from Brittany to Penzance each year, rented a store and rode their bicycles through the countryside, bunches of onions for sale hanging from their handle-bars. These were all people who came around the lanes of Mingoose in the sixties and into the seventies.

Although it was the road nearest to the coast, not many people seemed to find it in those days, even in summer. Nowadays it has become known as a short cut between Porthtowan and St Agnes, even though it is much steeper than the main road and has the very narrow bend. We are always expecting an accident on this corner. Sometimes in the summer we are in the garden and we hear a car coming down from the Victory Inn and another from the chapel. We stop whatever we are doing and hold our breath, waiting for the bang. But usually one car gets around the corner just before the other. Sometimes they meet head on, and if they can't brake in time headlights are smashed and wings dented.

The worst accident was to a motorcyclist who came off his

bike on the corner one night without any other vehicle being involved. A car came down from the inn, the driver saw the motorcycle and body and perhaps because he had just come out of the pub, he didn't want to get involved. He backed rapidly up the lane and hit another car coming down. He then, in some confusion, ran into our garden, thrust himself through the hedge and dropped about seven feet into the road. Meanwhile the motorcyclist was choking. It was this strange noise, loud enough to be heard through the stone walls, which had brought us out of the house, thinking it was some animal in distress. Pep pulled his tongue out of the back of his throat, turned him on his side and saved his life.

The hedge was thin where the motorist dropped through because an American army tank, training in Cornwall for the Normandy landings in the Second World War, hit the bank and knocked out several bushes. They were thrown over the wall into the field, where they still grow. The original hedge had nearly regained full thickness when a digger came down the lane with its arm swinging free. It pulled out the hedge by its roots again, and this time it was rebuilt with stones and a wooden fence.

It was at this spot that the corner's only fatality occurred, and it had nothing to do with traffic. It happened early in the nineteenth century, when the house was a 'kidley-wink'. A kidley-wink was licensed to sell beer and ale, but if you gave the landlord a wink, he'd probably find you a drop of contraband spirit concealed in the 'kidley' or kettle. A customer was going home drunk one

"'Ake, 'ake, fresh 'ake!" The fish-monger stops at the bottom of Mingoose Hill in the late nineteen-twenties, and Mrs Waters senior comes out to buy.

Ivy Cottage in the snow with
Rose Cottage behind it

night along the path at the side of the house. There was no fence then and he fell into the road. He was more unfortunate than the panicking driver, as the fall killed him. I think of him when I go by there in the dark, this local man, probably a miner, who sat drinking in our kitchen and then went through the back door and felt his way along the same stones that I feel if I haven't got a torch, over a hundred and eighty years ago.

When you live for long in one place, everywhere acquires associations. They might be tragic or comic or trivial, but they accumulate. This one insignificant corner has associations stretching from the beginning of the nineteenth century - it has an Ordnance Survey triangulation mark cut into one of the stones - to the Second World War and the present day. I do not think of them all, every time I go by, but they are always present.

Sometimes I see a stone in a bank or a bush in a hedge and I suddenly recall what I was thinking or feeling when I looked at it once before. The associations gathered around a house are much more complicated and it would be impossible to sort out all the thoughts and feelings that accompany it. I turn the corner and the house comes into view, like a child's drawing, a door with a window each side and three windows upstairs. On the stone walls are silver blobs of lichen like salt tear-stains. In winter the low trees in front of the house look as though the child has scribbled across the page, up and down with a thick pencil. It is the house where we have lived for nearly fifty years, where Susan, Frances and Stephen grew up and where Peter was born.

The layers are multiple. Even if only one or two are recalled in a passing glance, the rest are implicit. They give the place, the whole of the valley, a sort of resonance.

Cuba Downs

CHAPTER FIVE

Mingoose has more footpaths than roads. Some of them were once roads which were never adopted nor metalled and their use declined. The hedges filled with gorse and hawthorn that grew inwards, narrowing the way until they came to be used only by people on horseback or on foot. One such lane goes from the corner at the front of our house along the side of the garden and up to the coastal road. It is the quickest way for us to go to post, at the letter-box outside Towan Cross Farm. I hurry to catch the afternoon collection and then take my time walking back down the lane. The gorse hasn't been cut for a while and it almost meets in the middle; straight ahead is the Beacon. At a field gate, the path turns and descends to the house, through sycamore and ash trees. There are dead leaves underfoot and beneath the banks and trees it is very sheltered from the wind. Below are the grey slate roofs of the house and outbuildings, and beyond the house and its chimneys are the valley and the sea.

A man I met one day told me that he used to drive a horse-drawn butcher's van and that he came down the lane regularly, turning into the road at the bottom in front of the house. It would be impossible to drive anything through the lane now.

Another very narrow path links the road to the lane along the back of the garden, so that our house sits in an acute-angled triangle of ground, an island surrounded on all sides by public ways. This narrow path, deep between stone walls, is really a drain - a 'drang' or 'droke' - built to take the rainwater away from the house. The water pours off the hillside and at times the paths can be like streams. They can be muddy, too. I heard Mrs Rashleigh one day in the drang. She had been visiting in Mount Hawke and wore ordinary shoes. "Maister mud," she was saying, "I shall be glad to be rid of 'ee."

The large-scale Ordnance Survey map of 1907 shows nearly every field criss-crossed with footpaths. Most of them give access to the stream. There was a footpath from our house right through the middle of the garden at Wayside, which would then have been a field. It led to a chute where an iron pipe spouts water into the

Emily Tredinnick at the window of
Mingoose Cottage

stream. The Rashleighs still used it when we first came here. Mrs Rashleigh said it made a lovely cup of tea, much better than tap water, though it doesn't now pass any quality tests. It must have supplied several houses, because about four paths converge on it and it was a source for the water-carrier, who sold the water by the bucketful.

May Morrison used to walk these paths once a year to keep them open. Nobody uses them now or tries to preserve them as rights of way. They are no longer needed, as the water comes through the tap. When it was first piped to the hamlet, May's mother Emily Tredinnick would only have a tap outside the back door. That was luxury enough, she said, after having to carry water to Mingoose Cottage from the chute.

A wide track leads to the downs beyond the chapel, now converted to a dwelling, and beside Chapel Villa, rebuilt when the original thatched cottage was demolished. It was very like the derelict cottage in Scoll Lane and looked like an untidy haystack. It was lived in by an old man, Mr Oates, who had once been a miner. He had a regular corner behind the door in the Victory Inn, and most evenings we would hear him walking back from the pub with Mr Martin.

Edwin Tredinnick remembered a John Penrose living there, a big, harmless man who used to talk about imaginary things. He was committed to the asylum at Bodmin and Constable Benney came from St Agnes to supervise his removal. When he saw how big he was, he took out his truncheon and knocked him unconscious. John's wife, Harriet, rushed screaming down the road to Mingoose House. Eddie's father, James, disapproved of the policeman's action and told him so. 'He took him to task over it,' and the two men never liked each other after that. As Edwin tells the story, one can hear the tones of Victorian moral concern. James Tredinnick was a forthright character, speaking his mind to the bullying steward Coulter Hancock or the over-zealous local constable. (Benney's great-grandson Clive became a popular police sergeant and noted local historian living in the village today. In his version of the story his ancestor was followed from St Agnes by a large crowd expecting some excitement; they were disappointed by the speedy outcome.)

John Penrose never came back from Bodmin. Clifford Oates

was taken to the Epiphany Home in St Agnes. The house decayed still further, until it was sold, pulled down and a new house built in its place. The track at the side of it goes past stables and a large barn where beef cattle are wintered. A footpath leads through the yard and across the fields to Wheal Lawrence valley, though the track continues to Cuba Downs. The name is possibly another corruption of a Cornish word, though there might be a link with nearby Spain Downs. Until the nineteenth century it was all heath between St Agnes and Truro.

Cuba Downs is a moor of heather and short gorse, but part of it was once cultivated, as it is divided into fields by stone hedges. The land was broken during the First World War, but it hasn't grown anything since. It is used by Mount Hawke Gun Club and on the last Saturday of every month they hold a clay pigeon shoot. They used an old GWR van as a clubhouse until they built a new one. There are various stands for shooting from and the ground is littered with fragments of the discs. They fly a red flag when they are shooting. From the other side of the valley we hear a shout of "Pull" and then the shots from the double-barrelled guns, like the repeated slamming of doors. We see the clay pigeons lobbing up into the air above the top of the hillside and shattering to pieces. After the shoot our son Peter would earn some pocket money by collecting any undamaged discs.

The downs where the gun club meets is the site of what must have been one of the last small tin-mining ventures in Cornwall.

Wheal Mangle on the downs

In the nineteen-seventies millions of pounds were invested in Wheal Jane and Wheal Concord, and South Crofty near Camborne and Wheal Geevor near Lands End had been producing tin more or less continuously, though all are now closed. But in the nineteen-forties, Martin Yelland, claiming ancient tinners' rights, sank a shaft on the downs. According to these rights, a tinner can mine any ground he stakes a claim to, without any hindrance from the owner. He called it Wheal Noweth, the new mine, but it became known as Wheal Mangle, because the winding gear was adapted from an old mangle through which clothes used to be passed on washing day to squeeze out the water. He was helped by his father Joe Yelland and by Cliff Oates.

In an article in John Bull dated 16th October 1948, Harry Hopkins gives an account of his visit to the mine. "I climbed, rather shakily, down the rickety ladders. Above us the rust-brown kibble dangled in the square of blue sky.

"The fumes of dynamite hung about the bottom of the shaft. Yelland's son had been blasting again. In the morning he works at his trade as a watchmaker; in the afternoons he labours in Mangle Mine, drilling the hard rock, planting the dynamite, lighting the fuses, running up the ladders - then descending as the smoke rolls away, to get at the rock.

"It is tough work and slow work. The shaft is down twenty-five feet now, and so far nothing much has turned up. Another twenty-five feet and then, if there's still nothing, they'll try a crosscut."

A visitor to the mine poses in the tramway wagon, on which Martin had painted the Cornish coat of arms.

They went down about thirty feet before giving up. Martin was very non-committal about the amount of tin they found.

The track continues past several granite gate-posts that I coveted for many years. When the gun club blocked the field entrances and half-buried them in earth, I felt justified in making an offer. We had a digger to nudge them gently out of the ground and carry them to our gate. There they remained for two years while we tried to work out a way of carrying them to the top of the garden. Granite weighs about a hundredweight a square foot, so the largest post was nearly half a ton. We had lots of suggestions: winches, levers, slings; St Agnes Rugby Club, the Territorial Army, a helicopter from Culdrose. In the end we found a farmer with a tractor which was heavy enough to lift one at a time and small enough to go through narrow field gates. Each of the four stones was carried up to the Victory Inn, through Towan Cross, through fields and tracks and dropped over the bank into the garden.

I had dug holes ready to receive them, a group of three at the highest point and a single one lower down the slope. We manoeuvred them into position. The next day I decided that two of them needed to change places and Stephen and I swapped them over. It cost me a week in bed with a bad back. Placed upright they immediately became figures, a family group. They are very uneven in shape, with heads and shoulders. They have holes like giant eyes. The sides are notched where the 'feathers' split the granite open, and the surface has streaks of red like blood in the stone.

Martin Yelland at Wheal Mangle

A gatepost on Cuba Downs

The texture is weathered and lichen-covered.

Some posts still remain in the banks of the track across Cuba Downs. The downs once extended further, but in the nineteen-eighties farmers were paid subsidies to destroy hedges and reclaim heathland. For weeks a yellow and black digger, a JCB on caterpillar tracks, scraped laboriously away at the top soil, piling up heather and roots into heaps. These were set alight and burned slowly, the smoke drifting across the landscape. When the wind was in the right direction, the whole of Mingoose smelled of burning for day after day. At night the digger was parked on the skyline, its arm extended and its claw ready to pounce. It looked like a prehistoric monster or a creature from outer space. Walking across the moor through the smouldering piles was like walking into a film set.

Wheal Daisy

CHAPTER SIX

The most frequently used footpath in Mingoose is the one through the bottom of the valley to the sea. There has always been some uncertainty as to whether it was a footpath or a bridleway. Soon after coming here I referred to it as a bridleway, possibly because it sounded more 'country life', and was told very sharply that it was a footpath. It was marked as a footpath on the definitive map drawn up after the end of the war. The British Horse Society applied for the path to be upgraded to a bridleway and the council made the order. There were objections, principally from the National Trust which owns most of its length, and a three-day enquiry was held in the Scout Hall in St Agnes.

Some parts of the path give access to the mines and are wide enough for a horse and cart. Other lengths in between are no more than a foot wide, at one spot with a sheer drop to the stream below. Riders have always used the path to reach the sea. The enquiry was not concerned with suitability or safety; all that mattered was whether it had been used. The horse-riders seemed to have a good case.

But the National Trust argued that they never intended to allow unrestricted horse-riding and they had shown that intention by having a licensing system, even though it had lapsed after a few years. They offered an alternative route and had always allowed free access on the moors. The inspector found against the modification order. It is now officially a footpath, but the dispute has probably not ended yet.

Just below our back gate, another green and white signpost says PUBLIC FOOTPATH. At the enquiry many riders when cross-examined denied ever seeing it. The path is as wide as a lane at first and tempts some large vehicles to enter it. A council refuse lorry drove down it once, its offside wheels went over the edge and it hung above the garden of Wayside. A bigger lorry came to pull it out.

The trees on our side of the path had Dutch elm disease and I cut them down. There were some tall pines on the other side, which were blown down in the great gales. The lane crosses the

41

Mrs Rashleigh with Cindy at the door of her chalet

Mrs Rashleigh and her blind cow Tina on Mingoose Hill, followed by Shep

stream to Mingoose Vale, a cottage under the hill beneath the gun shoot. It was where Mr and Mrs Rashleigh lived when we first came here. They had a few cows, pigs and chickens, and Jack hired himself out for farming and gardening at five shillings an hour. After his death from pneumonia, his daughter and her husband moved into and modernised the house, and Mrs Rashleigh moved into a chalet at the bottom of the steep field.

Here she lived with her two dogs, surrounded by her chickens, ducks and geese. The ducks would waddle up to the top of the field and hurtle down at full speed, launching into the air and just managing to land on the ridge of the roof. The hens scratched in the dust beneath the chalet. Lying all around were feeding troughs and old tyres turned inside out for water, and pens and nesting boxes that she knocked together out of corrugated iron, old wood and wire netting. She was continually repairing and strengthening them against the foxes, which lay in wait in the gorse bushes on all sides of the field. They would even come out in broad daylight to carry off a duck or a hen. She spoke of 'God's creatures' and treated them all with great charity. But the fox was an exception. "Maister Fox," she called him, and always added, "the varmint."

One Saturday morning when her daughter and son-in-law were out, she set light to the gorse to destroy the foxes' cover. Cornish farmers have always burnt off the gorse in this way. But there was a strong south-westerly wind blowing and the gorse was very dry. It blazed like kindling and in no time great sheets of flame were leaping into the sky. It was terrifying how quickly it took hold. Mrs Rashleigh went down to her chicken huts and made herself busy feeding her hens.

In the wind, the flames spread rapidly up the hillside. The gorse burnt with a loud crackling noise. The fire reached a hedge and moved along it towards the nursery. Clouds of black smoke billowed upwards above the flames. The men from the nursery came out with shovels and tried to beat it back, to make a gap between the furze and their plastic tunnels. The smoke swirled around them. The siren of a fire-engine sounded in the distance, getting nearer and nearer. Mrs Rashleigh pottered on for a while, then disappeared inside the chalet and closed the door.

The fire-engine came down from the Victory Inn, through Mingoose and up to the chapel. It took the track to the gun shoot and came out on the downs above the fire, which was now advancing through the heather. A second bright red appliance came over the top and through the smoke. It stopped on the slope and half a dozen firemen in yellow waterproofs got out and started to beat the flames. Some of them reeled out hoses. The fire still flared up in places, but they soon had it under control. The hillside cleared and it seemed very quiet after all the drama. Mrs Rashleigh opened her door again.

She lived close to her animals, in a way of life which hadn't changed much since the Middle Ages. Inevitably, with her cockerels and hens and her battles with 'Maister Fox', she recalled the widow who nearly lost Chauntecleer to the fox in Chaucer's Nun's Priest's Tale:

A povre wydwe, somdeel stape in age
Was whilom dwellyng in a narwe cotage,
Biside a grove, stondynge in a dale.

She stopped getting her water from the chute above the stream. She had electricity and a radio and television, and collected her old-age pension. But in essentials this sort of country life had gone on for hundreds of years.

She always looked the same, neither old nor young, in all the time that we knew her. Her health was good, though once she cracked some ribs; her grandson-in-law couldn't start his car and she gave it a push to jump it in. She was a tiny lady, standing about twice the height of her cow dog Cindy. She always spread her washing in the old Cornish fashion on the gorse bushes along the stream.

The path to Mingoose Vale in the nineteen-twenties

Mingoose Vale and
Mrs Rashleigh's chalet

When I used to see her in her raincoat and yellow wellies - which she called 'bombades' - hammering away in the rain at one of her chicken huts while Cindy stalked a goose on the hillside, or when I heard her calling in her cats or singing a hymn, I thought of her many contemporaries in old people's homes and hospital wards. Mrs Rashleigh had a good old age.

The lane crosses the stream to Mingoose Vale, but the footpath continues down the valley on the left bank, past a gate marked FLORAL COTTAGE. The fields on both sides have been planted as a wood, with ash, sycamore and sweet chestnuts, and with pine trees as a wind-break at the seaward end. They were planted by Mickey Dale, a semi-retired doctor from the Midlands who worked part-time at the Newquay surgery. He said that he was growing trees because they wouldn't need much attention. Often when I drew the bedroom curtains in the morning I would look out and see him already at work in his bright yellow waterproof, clearing the grass and weeds between the trees. They grew quickly and now they are being coppiced by his successor.

The path alongside the wood passes between may-thorn and sloe bushes that meet overhead. It looks like one thick hedge from above, but there is a tunnel through the middle of it. It is always very muddy, as there is no sun or air to dry it out and no drains to take the water away. It emerges on to the hillside, keeping more or less to the contour line. The stream descends over small falls, some way below amongst the willows whose tops are level with the path. There is a glimpse of water between the tree trunks and the stream often floods. In spring there are wild daffodils. Above the path, the hillside is covered with heather and gorse.

To walk along here with Martin Yelland was to see it as it was over a hundred years ago, when the mines were working. He knew of nineteen mines that had been active in Mingoose or the immediate vicinity and he reckoned that several hundred people worked here. There was a shaft beneath the sycamore tree, by the side of the stream a little further down. There were levels going into both hillsides and adits to drain water from the mines. A tramway came out of one level and trucks tipped the ore down the slope.

The bal-maidens worked with hammers, smashing the rocks into smaller lumps before the ore went into the stamps to be crushed

The mine in the valley at the turn of the century. Today there is no trace of the workings, and the area is covered with vegetation.

to sand. The stamps were worked by water-wheels (there were five of them in the valley when Mr Tredinnick was a boy). They pounded the stones night and day and the noise filled the air. The people of Mingoose were so used to it that they would wake up if it stopped in the night. There were buddles, round tanks in the ground where the tin settled. The pathway then was wide enough for horses and carts to pass up and down, carrying the tin away to be smelted.

He would point out features of the landscape which seemed overgrown and meaningless, and give them significance. A horseshoe-shaped scar on the opposite slope, with a level platform in front of it, was where the mine foreman had lived in a wooden bungalow. I pictured it as a shack out of a shanty town in the Far West or during the gold rush in Australia. In the hillside behind is an opening like a cave, except that it doesn't go back any distance. It once had a heavy door across the front, with a large padlock. It was the dynamite store for the mine.

It looks as though a footpath ran along the other side of the valley, level with the path to Chapel Porth. In fact, this is the course of an old leat, which took water from Mingoose around the hillside into Wheal Lawrence, where water was less plentiful and the stream sometimes dried up in summer, bringing the stamps there to a halt. There were more battles between miners over water and the power that it provided than there have ever been over footpaths and bridleways. They must have paid a fee or tribute for its use. Sections of the leat are still recognisable, a water channel now over-grown with bracken.

The path widens slightly, where a bit of the hillside has collapsed, washed out perhaps by the rainwater though it hardly merits a second glance. Martin said that this was the turning point. The mine in the bottom of the valley had a horse-whim, not a fire-whim; it didn't have a steam engine to provide the power to 'bring the ore to grass'. There was a winding gear over the shaft and a horse was attached to a rope that passed over a pulley. As the horse was driven along the path it drew up the kibble or bucket from the bottom of the mine. This point was where the horse stopped; the bucket had reached the top. It was emptied, and the boy turned the horse and led it back to the shaft, lowering the kibble to the bottom again. The distance between where we stood and the sycamore tree is the distance from top to bottom of the shaft. I measured it out along the path, one hundred and sixty paces.

I went one evening with him into the level in the opposite hillside. We crossed the stream, the children with us, and pushed our way up through the gorse and bracken, until we came to an entrance. It had been hidden by a mound of rubble and earth tipped in front of it. This had grown over, covering the small opening that remained at the top. We parted the fronds and brambles, and saw a pit sloping inwards. We slid down the earth, feeling like foxes entering a burrow. It was dark inside and the children were frightened. Martin felt around for the acetylene lamp he kept there. He used to spend a lot of time wandering around underground, in all the mines of the district.

The lamp lit up the tunnel. We could stand upright, though the walls weren't quite vertical. The tunnel slanted to one side, where the lode had been at an angle. He said that the one slanting inwards was the 'hanging' wall and the other was the 'foot' wall. Both walls glistened with damp, the lamp hissed and our breath steamed before us. The floor under our feet was packed firm, with sleepers every yard or so where the tramway had run, though the rails had been taken up.

This was Wheal Daisy. It had been worked by tributers, independent miners who weren't paid a wage, but rewarded according to the amount of tin they brought to the surface. In a good week they could do better than a wage earner, but in a bad lode they could do much worse. Often mines were called after abstract virtues, like Wheal Liberty, Wheal Unity or Wheal Friendship, or after the mine-captain's wife, like Wheal Kitty, Wheal Gertrude or Wheal Charlotte. But this mine hadn't been named after a woman called Daisy. They had given it the name because they worked the lodes so near the surface that they said they could see the daisy roots hanging down from above.

We went on through the level until we came to a stope. This was where the miners, following a vein of tin, had cut upwards and away from the level, filling in with pit props as they went. These not only supported the sides, but gave them a platform from which to attack the rock. The reverse of a stope, when they cut downwards from a level, was called a winze. The light penetrated only part of the way up the stope; there was a suggestion of cavernous depths beyond. We put out the lamp and lit a candle, to see it as the miners had seen it. The candle flickered on the brown walls, illuminating a limited area and throwing into sharp relief all the sharp edges of rock. We imagined the men working in this semi-darkness, climbing up the stope on the wooden beams towards the roots of the daisies.

We went on past other stopes, pushing deeper into the hillside. There was a hole drilled for dynamite, but it hadn't been blasted. We came to some crumbling blue-grey rock. "This is what we call

The workforce at Wheal Daisy about 1910. The ladies have put on their furs for the photographer.

47

peachy. If you were prospecting and you came to this, you'd know there was tin not far away. It's what we call 'turning country'."

Then we reached a fall of rock, where some of the roof had collapsed. The pit props had rotted; one was lying across the tunnel and as I stepped on it the bark tore and it squelched under my heel. The wood was pink like tinned salmon. Martin had a hammer with him and he tapped the walls. There was a gap between the roof and the fallen rock, and on his own he would have wriggled through and gone on another hundred yards into the hill. But I wouldn't take the children any further.

It was getting dark when we came out. Pep was at the front gate looking for us, and she saw the lights on the opposite hillside and the figures moving across the downs, like miners of the past coming home from their 'core'.

The Valley

CHAPTER SEVEN

The sycamore tree marks the site of the mine in the bottom of the valley. The tree is not growing there by chance; it was almost certainly planted by the miners when they abandoned the shaft. It was their habit to leave a tree, often an elder, to mark the spot. There is no other sign now of an eighty-fathom drop, only a deep hollow in the ground beneath the spreading branches. The shaft was not filled; it was probably capped and the usual way was to fell a small tree and throw it in. The branches would be springy enough to hold against the sides of the shaft, and then it would be topped with rubble and earth.

Obviously this method does not offer much security, especially after a few decades. The branches lose their elasticity, and rot. The layer of earth sits across the top of the shaft, with nothing but habit and perhaps a few roots to hold it in place. The hollow beneath the sycamore would once have been level, so the plug of earth and stone has dropped several feet. It wouldn't take much of a shake for it to fall right through.

This often happens in mining areas and several shafts have opened up suddenly, usually overnight, in St Agnes. The only mine cap to have collapsed in Mingoose was in our garden, before we came here. The first we heard of it was when we were living in one of Mr Jolly's chalets in Porthtowan, while we were waiting to move into Mingoose Villa. Monty the butcher called one day. "You know there's a shaft in the garden?" he asked.

We didn't know and we questioned the two ladies, Miss Crewes and Miss English, who lived in the house. They told us what had happened. They had known nothing about the mine. They only knew that behind the outbuildings was a sun-trap, sheltered on one side by the wall and on the other by a semi-circle of terraces. They were sitting there in deck-chairs one fine spring morning during the war. It must have been the 20th May 1941, following an air raid the previous night. The target was the aerodrome at Nancekuke, where Ernie Landry was trying to farm, longing for foggy days to keep the planes from flying. (The cattle got used to them, but the horses never did.) Some of the bombs fell on

Porthtowan beach, the beach was mined and some of the landmines exploded. One bomb fell on Cuba Downs behind the chapel, leaving a crater which gave Martin Yelland the idea of sinking his shaft.

The ladies went in for lunch. When they came out afterwards the deck-chairs had disappeared and where they had been sitting was a gaping hole. The bombing during the night had shaken the earth and dislodged the plug. They were shocked by their narrow escape.

After the war the shaft was capped by the Duchy of Cornwall, which owns all the mineral rights on this side of the stream; on the other side they belong to the Enys estate. They capped it by digging down to rock, placing a pre-war car chassis across it and topping off with six feet of concrete. It is still a sun-trap and a good place to set up a table for lunch in the summer. There's no feeling that you are on top of a mine. An ash tree leans over it (planted by the miners when they first plugged the shaft?) and all around are the walled terraces growing with ferns and montbretia. It's a natural amphitheatre, a sort of miniature Minack, and when Sue and Fran were young they used to put on summer concerts here, shows with singing and dancing and improvisations. I sit over the shaft without any qualms and then I suddenly remember the thin skin of concrete and the drop of a hundred fathoms. I look at the fissures in the floor. The ants are crawling in and out, but the cracks don't look any wider.

I wouldn't, however, walk across the earth hollow above the

The valley in about 1920, showing East Wheal Charlotte and Chapel Porth Farm

shaft in the valley, but I did go there once when I was looking for some stolen property. We have a small field on the other side of the road, with a few fruit trees and a vegetable patch. An old chicken house is built of cement blocks and roofed with corrugated iron. It has a plastic fertiliser bag nailed across the window, as the glass has gone, and no door. There are a lot of little sheds like this in the fields of Mingoose, made of brick or blocks, wood or corrugated iron. They are overgrown with ivy, surrounded by nettles and brambles, almost disappearing into banks and hedges. They are mostly disused and dilapidated. Ours was last used as a play house. The children painted the walls with emulsion and even put up some wallpaper, though that soon curled in the damp. They hung curtains and had boxes for furniture.

Breakfast on the mineshaft at Mingoose Villa

Later, I kept a few garden tools there. If a tool I wanted wasn't there, I assumed I'd taken it up to the house. If it wasn't at the house, I assumed it was in the field. Gradually it dawned on me that several were missing.

I remembered seeing some boys in the lane, hanging about suspiciously. We made a few enquiries - or rather, Pep did, as she is good at that sort of thing - and the word must have gone round because one Saturday morning the phone rang and it was the father of two of the boys. The older boy was away on holiday, but the younger brother had told the whole story. The tools were in an adit in the valley. The boy was too scared to go there on his own and bring them to the house and the father was in bed with 'flu, so Peter and I went to look for them.

It was a damp day, not actually raining, but misty and everywhere was soaking. There were drops of moisture on the grass and on the prickles of the gorse bushes, giving a grey sheen to everything. You could just make out the sea, but there was no horizon. The stream rushed noisily through the valley.

The boy's father had said the adit was close to the footpath, so it wasn't Wheal Daisy. I knew of an opening just above the path, level with the sycamore marking the shaft, but when we got there we could see where they had been going down a steep path to the hollow under the tree. They had cut gorse bushes to cover their tracks. We moved them aside and there was a rope tied to a thick stump of gorse, so that we could hold on to it and let ourselves down. We stood at the edge of the depression. They had hung a rope over an arm of the sycamore, on which they had been swinging from one side to the other. Cautiously, we worked our way around the hollow and over a bank. A few feet away the stream was roaring over a drop amongst the rocks. In the hillside was an opening that we had never seen before. It was entered through a trench that had been walled with stone, and there was a lintel over the mouth of the tunnel. It must have been hidden by gorse and brambles, which the boys had cleared. They had used flat stones to pave the entrance.

Inside it was very dark and we hadn't brought a torch. We went into the blackness and turned round, beginning to see not only the square of light but some of the interior. It was cut out of the rock, not quite high enough to stand upright. It had probably drained water into the stream from Charlotte United Mine on the top of the hill.

It made a good den, though everywhere was running wet. The air we breathed seemed chill and heavy with moisture. The boys had some maps there and the paper had already gone soft and limp. They had two lamps and a gallon of paraffin, candles, cups and tins, and lots of test tubes in wooden racks. Against the wall, well back in the dark, were my pickaxe, spade, fork and bow-saw.

The local children always played in the valley and on the beach, with a freedom that would alarm modern parents. It was a dangerous playground. Boys would ride their bicycles around the mouths of open shafts. They would toboggan down the slope of Mulgram Hill at Chapel Porth on pieces of driftwood picked up from the beach. They would dare each other to be the last to jump off before the plank plunged over the edge of the cliff. With fathers working in the mines, some of them had access to dynamite, even though it was supposed to be kept behind heavily-locked doors. A favourite sport was blowing up rocks, and Eddie Tredinnick recalled how he and his friends sent a boulder on the cliffs sailing through the air and falling half a mile out to sea with a satisfying splash.

Peter and I collected the tools, edged gingerly around the shaft and carried them back up the valley. The boy's father was a fisherman and he said that when the older boy returned he'd get him to dress a crab for us and bring it to the house, but we are still waiting.

Beyond the adits and the mines and the ledges of rubble where nothing grows, there is another opening in the hillside, larger than

The path down the valley in the
nineteen-thirties, little changed today

all the others and right at the side of the path. It looks as though it
had something to do with the mines, though there's no shaft. Martin
believed it was where the stone was quarried for our house. It is
the same brown slate-stone and there is a level track along which
the carts could have passed. He knew for certain that a similar
quarry in the hillside beneath the gun shoot was where all the stone
for the chapel came from, so it seemed reasonable to suppose that
the quarry on this side of the valley provided the stone for Mingoose
Villa. It seems about right for size. If I look back from here, I can
imagine a sort of time-lapse film taking place in the first decade of
the eighteen-hundreds, with the hillside breaking away and shooting
up the valley to re-erect itself in the form of a house with four
walls, a door in the front, a window on each side and three windows
above. I can then reverse the film and the house collapses, flows
down the valley and returns to the hillside.

From this spot it is the only house that is visible, standing
right in the middle between two hillsides. It juts out from one side,
not horizontally, but seeming to lean with the slope of the hill. It is
surrounded by trees which are gradually obscuring it.

The path drops from here, going down through bracken to
the level of the stream, and the narrow valley widens. The sea is
still there at the end and the Beacon has come into view again. The
land slopes down from the Beacon to Wheal Lawrence valley, with
a cluster of chalets on the road to Chapel Porth. A grass field lies
in the bottom of the valley, with a low wood on the slope. In winter

East Wheal Charlotte in winter

the ivy-covered walls of two derelict cottages can be seen amongst the trees, and there was another end wall in the field beyond, but that has now been levelled. Although the field has been ploughed and re-sown, the course of the leat is still visible where it went around the brow into the next valley. In a corner of the bottom field, the same JCB dug a pond with an island in the middle. The water reflects the chalets on top of the hill.

The western side of the valley has no fields, only bracken which is green and tall in summer and fox-red for the rest of the year until the new shoots uncurl their fronds. The engine house of East Wheal Charlotte stands above a mound of rubble. We can see it when we lie in bed and look down the valley. Depending on the light, it either stands out clear against the hillside, usually in the early morning, or merges into the background later in the day. It is built of stone and has no roof. The chimney stack is finished with brick and a few layers have fallen. It looks as though someone has taken a bite out of it.

A track passes across the hillside and there are one or two burrows, mine tips which spill out into the heather. They have a pinkish tinge and the burrows and walled shafts of Wheal Charlotte stand out against the sky. At the bottom is the junction with the footpath from Wheal Lawrence valley. Another path climbs up to Wheal Charlotte moor and the Victory Inn. These paths mark, I suppose, the limits of Mingoose, but I normally would never stop here. I would continue straight along the path through Chapel Coombe to the beach.

The Beach

CHAPTER EIGHT

Alongside the stream is a small wood, and behind it were the Chapel Porth riding stables of Virginia Landry. The engine house is now high up on the left. Some years ago, a hole appeared in the path beneath. I dug at it with the heel of my boot until I could see water below. The adit from the main shaft to the stream was collapsing and later the National Trust put a wooden bridge over it.

Beyond the bridge, the character of the landscape changes from an inland to a coastal valley, even though the sea has temporarily disappeared from view. There is no more bracken, only heather and gorse growing close to the ground. The smell of salt is in the air. The path is stony underfoot and in winter forms one of the channels of the stream, which it now closely follows. There is a lot of evidence of mining activity, with a wall sticking out from the other side of the valley where a water-wheel worked the stamps, part of the Old Century tin works.

Above them is a dry water-course or 'girt', one of several in the valley. They developed at the end of the Ice Age, when much more water was flowing off the hills. It is marshy around the stream and the view ahead is blocked by a bank of earth. I come up on to this bank and am hit by the wind blowing in from the sea. Ahead, a few hundred yards away, is the sea itself, usually with tier upon tier of breakers between the steep sides of the cove.

The bank was part of an American Army tank-training course. The tracks already on the hillside, used by mules to bring the ore in panniers from Wheal Charlotte down to the stamps in the valley, were too steep; the army bulldozed a track across the slope and put a wooden bridge over the stream. The American bridge - Blackman's bridge some called it (for many it was the first time they had seen black people) - was dismantled after the war, but the banks up to it remain.

From here I soon come to the beach, crossing the stream into the car park. This was once full of workings, right up to the shore. There was a blowing house for smelting in the centre and a water-wheel to work stamps on the site of the present toilets. A

The Old Century tin works in the lower part of the valley

The Old Century tin works about 1920

buddle was a pit in which the crushed ore from the stamps was washed in water to separate the tin from the impurities, on the same principle as a panning shovel. As the water swirled round, the tin being heavier was deposited more quickly than other particles. There were several buddles between the blowing house and the sea-wall, built to hold back the spring tides. Only the high retaining wall of the water-wheel remains. In summer there used to be huts for the car park attendant and lifeguards until a building was made right in the hillside. A mast flies a red flag when bathing is unsafe, and below it are red and white signs, summer and winter, saying DANGEROUS BEACH.

When Mr Retallack's grandmother Winnie Rickard became a widow early in the last century and had to make a living, her uncle Joe Tremewan built a wooden chalet on the hillside and she sold teas. "You couldn't do that now," said Mr Retallack. "They wouldn't let you. You can't do this and you can't do that, Mingoose is what I call 'religious' country, you can't do anything."

There were one or two chalets on the slopes, but they were cleared by the National Trust with all the old workings when they acquired the cove in 1956 and the following year they built a discreet stone and slate tea-house. Here through the sixties and seventies Mrs Jean Donald served beach teas; the teapot, milk jug and china crockery were packed into a wooden box with a handle, and carried down to the sand. It seemed a quaint survival belonging more to the period of Mr Retallack's grandmother. The tea-house

Chapel Porth beach, c1905

Chapel-Porth, Nr. Porthtowan

ABOVE
The Porth in 1957 after it had been acquired by the National Trust.
LEFT
The remains of industrial activity at the beach, with Rickard's Tea Rooms on the left

was burned down in the eighties and replaced by a larger building. At the same time the stream was channelled between stone banks and a sea-wall built of granite with cobbles on the top.

On the hillside the name CHAPEL PORTH is spelt out in white pebbles. They were first put there by scouts from a camp in 1911, but at various times they have been rearranged into HAPPY XMAS, into a hammer and sickle in 1968 and a large NO when the coastal footpath was closed during the foot and mouth crisis. They were often changed into people's names and initials or rolled down to the beach, but Robin Ross from the café always puts them back and repaints them. The National Trust tolerates it, reluctantly one feels.

A 'porth' is where a river or stream enters the sea, and it was called Chapel Porth after a chapel which once stood here, in the raised valley on the east side of the cove leading towards Wheal Coates. There was a holy well or spring some fifty yards from the edge of the cliff, with a small Gothic building above it. The antiquarian William Borlase sketched it around the middle of the eighteenth century, measured it (it was about eight feet wide and ten feet long) and gave a detailed description of it. It was built of moorstone which is 'extremely hard for tools, yet is the arch much eaten by the spray', and had a gabled roof. The water flowed into a square bowl of stone, with two niches for holy statues above, and there were stone benches on either side.

He noted on the plaster work 'some thousands initial letters of ye names of persons who thought to leave some memorandum

The caves in the cliffs at Porth, St Agnes

ABOVE
Icicles formed by the stream falling into the cave
RIGHT
The two vugs or caves below the hanging valley where the Chapel and well-house once stood

behind them, but were much mistaken, so near upon another are the letters.' He observed too that 'wanton fools' had torn down stones from the arch and sides. It survived for another seventy years, when some miners or farmers took the last stones away for hedging. When rebuked, they replied that a well was no use without water. The mining at Wheal Coates had drained the source of the spring.

The sketch made by Borlase has often been reproduced - it is on the Trust's information panel on the café wall - but it is not the chapel which gave its name to the porth; it was a well-house. The name derived from an early-mediaeval chapel which was destroyed during the Reformation and remained a ruin until its final removal in 1780. There are no records of how it looked and some confusion over where it was sited. The Ordnance Survey maps of 1881 and 1908 place it in the corner of the present car park, where the café now stands. There is no evidence for this and it was probably near the well in the hanging valley.

This valley was described as a 'dingle' or 'dingle-combe' by Victorian writers, who romanticised the chapel and well, inventing a solitary who prayed for sailors at sea and gave assistance to shipwrecked mariners. It is a fantasy which I find attractive and lying awake at night during a gale, listening to the wind howling and the rain lashing, my mind goes out to the hermit in his stone cell above the raging waves of Chapel Porth.

The water from the well was described by Borlase as 'very

ABOVE
The Morrison family camping at
Chapel Porth in 1927
LEFT
Chapel Porth in the thirties, showing
the remains of the water wheel

smooth and pure and has done wonderful cures'. In the eighteen-eighties the vicar of St Agnes, the Reverend Alfred Ruddall, wrote to the Reverend S. Baring-Gould: 'The spring does not now rise to the surface, but streams over the wall of a cavern which is accessible at half-tide. The water is beautifully cool and sweet, and is a great convenience and refreshment to visitors to the porth. They either put their lips to the little projections of the rocks and drink, or make little spouts of paper, and fill glasses or bottles.' It is a charming picture.

The stream spreads out across the beach. There are headlands on each side, Mulgram Hill to the south-west, its slope ending in a cliff with the profile of Queen Victoria, and White Rocks to the north-east, less sheer and with an outcrop of stones at the top like a natural castle.

The sea is nearly always rough on this coast. The waves come in like express trains and their roaring fills the cove. Surfers ride their boards, twisting and turning to keep ahead of the crest and in summer children swim and paddle in the shallows, in the area marked out by the lifeguards. It tends to be used by visitors; it has never been the beach of the people of St Agnes. It was too open to the Atlantic on the western side of the Beacon and it was further away than their own sheltered Trevaunance.

In the summer of 1927 the Morrison family camped here for a week. They put up three tents in what is now the car park and which was then hummocky sand covered with short grass. The

The profile of the western cliff, now less pronounced

water-wheel was still in place, with the drum for the stamps. There were not many visitors, as Bill remembered, and they had the run of the beach. The children would mark the sand into four sections with their spades, a quarter of the cove each for brothers Tim and Bill, sister Kath and their cousin.

Nowadays in August there are many more people. The car park soon fills and late-comers have to return to the overflow park at the top of the hill opposite the chalets. The early families take possession of the bays amongst the rocks. Others use wind-breaks to stake out claims to patches of sand. Sometimes, especially when the tide is well in, there is no sand to be seen. It is covered in the bright colours of striped canvas and beach clothes. The smell of sun-tan lotion comes over the sea-wall.

In the autumn the number of visitors decreases. The November gales create mountainous seas. From the shore the waves are piled storey upon storey and there is no other horizon, only the jagged, broken line of the crest. They pound the beach and the water is brown with suspended sand. In a November storm of 1928, Ernest Landry came along the cliff path from Porthtowan. He saw the stricken Eltham below and he knew what he wanted. The first two letters were his own initials and he was determined to have them. The waves were breaking over the boat, but he managed to reach it. With a screwdriver he wrenched off the solid brass E, but the L was more stubborn. The tide was coming in and some of the waves were breaking over him as he clung to the stern. Eventually a wave knocked him into the water and he struggled ashore. He never got the L to complete his initials. The next day the boat had broken up and the letters of the name had disappeared.

The storms strip the cove of its sand and for the rest of the winter it remains bare and stony, its rock exposed.

Wrecking

CHAPTER NINE

The Eltham was a Liverpool coaster of 687 tons, built by the Dublin Dockyard Company and launched in 1915. Her master was Ellis Foulkes of Connah's Quay, and she was bound from Swansea to Rouen with a cargo of coal. She was found beached and derelict just off the western headland of the cove, on the morning of the 18th November, 1928. There had been a north-westerly gale during the night, but no signals had been sighted by the coastguards, though empty flare and rocket cases were later found on the beach. There were some reports of mysterious lights which were thought to have been lightning. She soon broke in two. A boat was washed in at Chapel Porth, another at Perranporth, but the bodies of the crew were never found.

The boiler is still visible at low tide, lying half out of the sand. The holiday-makers paddle out to it and stand, king of the castle, on top. The waves break over the black iron, studded with rivets. It is only during a low spring tide that it is surrounded by sand. It serves as a marker: if I can see the boiler, I probably have time to walk under the cliffs past Black Angel rock to Porthtowan before the tide comes in.

Although the Eltham was the only boat wrecked at Chapel Porth, this stretch of coast has always had a lot washed up on it. One summer Peter and his friend Jem saw an aluminium beer barrel floating in the water. They ran into the sea to get it out, a wave came and they ran back. Each time they ran in they were driven back, but the waves were bringing the barrel closer and eventually they grabbed it. It was marked Irish Breweries Ltd and was half-full of either beer or sea-water. They played around with it for a while, rolling it about and standing on it, and then they were told that they would get twenty pounds for it from a brewery. They manhandled it all the way up the hill, rolling and carrying it, until they got to Jem's house. They phoned Devenishes - who weren't interested.

I like the idea of beachcombing, but I've never found anything very valuable. I've brought home a few planks of driftwood, which I've sawn up for the fire. If it's been in the sea long and impregnated

Rough seas at Chapel Porth

61

The wreck attracts a crowd, including the photographer, S. H. Richards, who had a newsagent's shop in St. Agnes.

with salt, it burns with a blue flame, and jumps and spits. The usual debris along the high-water mark is a collection of polystyrene bits and plastic bottles, lumps of tar, water-logged fruit - nearly always grapefruit - an electric bulb unbroken by the waves, small pieces of wood, frayed rope, lengths of fishing net and paint-brush handles without the bristles. More interesting is the natural flotsam like jellyfish and the egg-purses of skate. Sometimes there are the bones of cuttle-fish and strands of the seaweed eel-grass, which has probably drifted from the Isles of Scilly. Goose barnacles cling to beads of tar, pieces of wood and rope. Some summers the beach is littered with By-the-Wind-Sailors. More plastic, I thought, on first seeing the heaps of whitish material. But when I looked closer I could see the plastic-like sails which have carried the hydroids in vast flotillas all the way from the South Atlantic.

The current sweeps along the coast from the south-west. In the past it deposited quite useful finds on the beaches. Timber was plentiful in the days when it was carried as deck cargo, and I have heard of loads of coconuts washed up, the flesh still perfect inside the shell. Once, in the early years of the last century, a lot of candles came ashore. They could be picked up by the sackful and lasted many families for years. Wreckage like this was supposed to be handed over to the coastguards. The finder would be paid salvage money, but the amount did not make it worth the trouble. There were coastguards at Portreath and St Agnes, but the old hands at beachcombing never bothered with the main beaches. They

"s.s. Eltham" wrecked at Chapel Porth, Nov. 1928.

concentrated on the quieter places, where they reckoned there was no need to hand over what they found.

The coastguards, too, could sometimes be persuaded to turn a blind eye to what was going on. Ernest Landry used to beachcomb all along this stretch of the coast. He said that the coastguards knew what to do with a good swede, turnip or flatpole cabbage, a cart-load of farmyard manure tipped in a convenient place for their gardens, or when business was particularly brisk, a pound or two of farmhouse butter or a nice bit of fresh cream for Sunday tea.

Beachcombing reached its heyday during the First World War. Merchant ships were being torpedoed and all kinds of articles were washed up on the shore. The coastguards were called up for service and replaced by coast-watchers, young lads who were recruited locally from beachcombing families. There was no need to bribe them. When a Dutch ship ran on to a ridge off Godrevy, she broke up within hours and the cargo of sacks of flour was washed up the coast to be deposited between Porthtowan and St Agnes Head. The flour formed a paste around the inside of the sack, but in the middle it was quite dry. Hundreds of sacks were carried away in carts and a sack of the sifted flour was given to every old person in the area. The sacks were then turned inside out and the poultry fed on the paste that was sticking to the cloth. Nothing was wasted.

There were sides of cured ham, butter, lard and bacon, all undamaged by the sea-water, and barrels of lubricating oil, forty gallons to a barrel. The St Agnes coast-watchers took two barrels from Porthtowan beach and put them in a stable. The Portreath coast-watchers claimed they rightfully belonged to them and appealed to the beachcombers to do something about it. The 'wreckers' took two barrels that they had already drained and filled them with stream water, rubbing over the plug holes with thick oil and sand, so that no one would ever know they had been touched. Then they took the two barrels of oil from the stable and replaced them with the barrels of water. Everyone was satisfied: the Portreath coast-watchers had outwitted their St Agnes colleagues, the St Agnes coast-watchers sold the barrels, and the beachcombers had an extra eighty gallons of oil.

When bales of rubber were washed ashore, an official buyer paid cash for it, a pound a bale and no questions asked. There were hundreds of bales and some people made a lot of money. Many years later Frank Tompkins found a bale inside a cave at Chapel Porth. He thought at first it was made up of skins, but it was rubber from the same cargo. It was too heavy for him to move, so he asked Peter Landry, nephew of Ernest, to help. He had brought his bathing costume with him, as the entrance to the cave was waist-deep in water, but Peter Landry said that he intended to walk through without getting his feet wet. He took his crowbar and eased a few boulders here and there, and the water drained away. They shifted the bale up the valley and Frank thought it would be worth quite a lot, but they were never able to sell it.

Once between the wars large barrels of wine came ashore. They were too big to carry away and were broached on the spot.

The Eltham broken in two by the waves

Crowds rushed to Chapel Porth with jugs and basins, anything they could fill. A lot of people drank all they could and were rolling around the beach. It was pretty rough stuff.

Just after the war twelve tree-trunks of mahogany, ready-shaped for the sawmills, were washed up in the cove. The waves thrust one of them with such force into a cave that it jammed against the roof and there it stays to the present day. The other eleven were carted away. Another time there were hundreds of planks of Canadian pitch pine in the sea, but they weren't coming ashore. A gale arose during the night and when the planks were washed up on to the beach they had been reduced to matchwood.

One of the old beachcombers at Chapel Porth was Will Rogers. He was in the cave beneath Wheal Coates once, looking for wood from the galleries that the miners had left behind. Suddenly everything went black. He realised what had happened: an extra-large wave had filled the entrance, blotting out all the light. It came roaring towards him in the darkness. He leaped up to a ledge which he knew was above him and clung on with all his might as the water swirled around him.

The old men made no distinction between beachcombing and wrecking. They were grateful for any bounty that the sea cast up. To them, it was all 'wrecking', whether collecting cargo from a ship lost far out at sea or stripping a ship wrecked on the rocks. It never meant waving lanterns on the shore, to lure ships into danger. Such stories made them indignant; they said they were a slur on the Cornish. They never wanted a wreck to happen, but if it did,

An early photograph of the cliffs from Chapel Porth to St. Agnes Head

then they had every right to save what they could. If a ship was on the rocks, it would break up in a day or two and be no use to anyone. A rough tide or two would ruin any cargo and no one else would have been able to salvage it. The wreckers were only making use of what might otherwise have been wasted. They would risk their lives in the waves and spend perhaps a whole night soaked to the skin, carrying heavy planks or barrels up a steep cliff path. They only made a few shillings out of it. It was done more for the excitement than anything else.

But the Dutch captain of the Voorspoed, which ran aground in a northerly gale in Perran Bay on the 7th March 1901, didn't think the wreckers along this coast quite so harmless. The ship was looted and its contents, a general cargo including a stuffed alligator, carried off. The captain wrote later, "I have been wrecked in many parts of the globe, even in the Fiji Islands, but never among such savages as those of Perranporth."

A photograph was taken of the shipwreck by the Gibsons of Scilly. With its three masts still intact, it sits upright in the gleaming sand, while swarms of men and women climb over it like ants, or stand waiting with horses and carts. It looks like Gulliver, tied down by the Lilliputians. There are ladders and spars resting against the side, and the boys astride the spars are easing their way upwards.

A few years ago a stuffed alligator came up for sale in a local auction. I wonder if it was the one salvaged from the Voorspoed.

The Last of the Cornish

CHAPTER TEN

In the year when the Voorspoed was wrecked at Perranporth, James Tredinnick was living at Mingoose House. He had been born at Mingoose Cottage, across the paddock and down the hill, just as his father William had been. Working in the mines at fourteen and seeking work abroad when there was no employment locally, he had returned to his family rather than send for them to join him in California. He had enough money put aside to buy a lease on a comfortable house and small farm with three cottages to let. It was the traditional agreement based on three lives – and all three expired within a year. James was either very unfortunate or very unworldly; it was common to make one of the lives a distant relative in Australia, news of whose death would take a long time - if ever - to reach Cornwall. The Enys estate was known to be an understanding landlord and he was now paying a modest rent.

As well as the farm, in 1901 he had a butcher's shop opposite St Agnes post office. He was fifty-four years old, Emily was fifty-one. His family had been in the St Agnes area for seven generations, having come from Madron in the seventeenth century. Emily's family, the Tremewans, had also been in this part of the county for generations. All the houses in Mingoose at the turn of the century would have been occupied by families with a similar Cornish background.

In the same year, plans were well under way to bring the railway to St Agnes. There had been a Cornish main line for fifty years, but the line from Chacewater through St Agnes and Perranporth to Newquay was the last of the branch lines constructed in Cornwall by the Great Western Railway. In 1902 Edwin Tredinnick, James's youngest son, was thirteen years old. In the summer holidays he got a job on the building of St Agnes station at the far end of Scoll Lane. He made the tea and mixed cement, and was paid ten shillings a week. Unfortunately that summer the school-leaving age had been raised to fourteen. Ten shillings a week was a handsome sum and Eddie stayed on at work when the new term began. After a fortnight the whipper-in caught him, and James was fined ten shillings for not sending his son to school.

James and Emily Tredinnick at Mingoose House in 1910

St. Agnes station soon after
its opening in 1903

On the 6th July 1903 the railway line was opened as far as Perranporth and all the St Agnes schoolchildren were given a free trip. James had paid for his daughters to be privately educated at Mrs Harris's school for young ladies, at the bottom of Rosemundy Hill. Besides the basic lessons they learned elocution and drawing; they were all artistically gifted. James's youngest child, twelve-year-old Fanny May, walked along Scoll Lane that summer's morning to the railway station that her brother had helped to build. Eddie by now was working at Mr Moyle's blacksmith's shop next to the inn at Chiverton, where he saw his first motor car.

It was Fanny May's first ride on a train. There were to be many train journeys later, for the coming of the railway had a great effect on her life. It began to bring tourists to St Agnes. Some of them stayed at York House in British Road, just above the school, and in the summer of 1907 the landlady had more guests than she could sleep. She asked her friend Emily Tredinnick at Mingoose House if she would take in the Harvey family from London.

Fanny May was sixteen, and she had seen all the young men leaving to find work abroad. When the visitors were going, she asked Mr Harvey if he knew any nice young men in London to send down for her. Mr Harvey worked in a stockbroker's office and he must have spoken enthusiastically about his Cornish holiday, because the following year two young clerks from the office booked their stay at Mingoose House. James Tredinnick took the pony

The station under construction, 1902

and trap to the station to meet them. The newcomers had never heard a Cornish accent and couldn't understand a word that he said. James dropped them off at the front gate and led the pony along by the hedge of butcher's broom to the yard.

Three young women were watching from the window on the stairs, the round-arched window facing the road: Fanny May, her friend Ada Polglaze and Carrie. They hid behind the curtains and saw the young men coming up the garden path.

"I'll have the fair one!" said Fanny May.

And she did, although she had to wait six years before marrying him. The fair one was William Hume Morrison, whose family came from Scotland and who was nineteen years old. When Fanny May married him she went to live in Clapham, but returned at least once every year on the train to Mingoose House and later to Mingoose Cottage where her parents retired when James's sight began to fail.

Fanny May and Ada drive William Morrison into the yard at Mingoose House, c1910

I only knew her at the end of her life, when she had returned there to live. I used to see her sitting at her cottage window, and Susan interviewed her for her project. But in Bill Morrison's story of his parents' meeting she comes across as such a determined, lively young woman that it illuminates the whole of her life. When she was living in London, she always wanted to see every free show and parade that the city offered. "If we don't go," she would say, "we might as well be living in the middle of Mingoose Hill!"

Her three brothers also left Cornwall, following in their father's footsteps and seeking work in the United States. Herbert, who was thirteen years older than Edwin, had gone first, mining in Cripple Creek, Colorado, and later moving to Sacramento in California to work as a builder. When he was twenty Eddie decided to join him, and in 1909 with his brother Martin took the train to Southampton and sailed on the SS Teutonic. They could have travelled steerage for two pounds, but James, remembering no doubt his own crossing thirty years earlier, insisted on paying ten pounds each for their second-class fares to New York.

Within a year of their arrival Martin died from appendicitis. Eddie worked building railway bridges and bungalows, but in 1913 Emily wrote urging him to come home to help his father who was now almost blind. He returned and ran the farm, serving in the navy during the war, until his parents left Mingoose House in 1921

Ada Polglaze and Fanny May Tredinnick on the lawn in front of Mingoose House, c1910

to retire to James's birthplace. He was now free to return to the States. But other events intervened: he met Elsie Milman, a nurse at Truro City Hospital, and started to build his bungalow in Mingoose. The Cornish emigrant was often torn between his new country and his old, never certain that he had made the right choice. Eddie always wanted to go back to California, but it was not until after the Second World War that he sold up and sailed for America once more. He had left it too late; they couldn't settle and returned to St Agnes. His brother Herbert made his life in the States.

Susan wrote her project on Mingoose in 1969, when she was thirteen years old and a pupil at Truro Girls' Grammar School. It won a prize in the Cornish Gorsedd. As part of the project she made a survey of the population of the hamlet. She recorded seventeen properties with thirty-five inhabitants; in the 1851 census there had been two hundred and sixty-five. She looked at the age groups. She found seven children, four young adults aged 15-25, no one aged 25-35, eleven in the 35-45 group and thirteen aged 45 or over (a teenager's definition of old age). The youngest was three (her brother Peter) and the oldest were both seventy-eight. Carrie Yelland and May Morrison were born in the same year, 1891, and were generally thought to be sisters. They were in fact aunt and niece. James Tredinnick's wife Emily and his eldest daughter Winnie, seventeen years old and unmarried, were both pregnant at the same time. For a Methodist family in the eighteen-nineties it must have been very hard to bear. The two girls grew up as sisters and were as close as twins.

The revelation of the truth was like a scene from a Victorian novel. Aunt Morrison was visiting Mingoose House and one Sunday afternoon examined the family bible. "There's a mistake here," she exclaimed. "Carrie and Fanny May are born in the same year, with only three months between them. That must be wrong." There was a dreadful silence…

Poor Carrie, carrying all her life the stigma of being a 'base child'! Fanny May, lively and beautiful, married well and had three bright children. Carrie did not make a good match, thinking perhaps that she would never get a better offer. Joe Yelland had a moody temperament. He turned against his brother-in-law Eddie for marrying a foreigner, Elsie Milman from Plymouth, and would shout abuse at them as they walked up the hill to chapel. Their son

Martin was clever but odd.

Carrie had a hard life and deserved better. When I knew her in old age she was bent double, as though bearing a great weight. I sometimes accompanied Martin home. For a watchmaker he had surprisingly little sense of time and might be hours late for a meal, but Carrie would serve the pasty that she had been keeping hot for him in the Cornish range. When James had a stroke and was completely blind and paralysed, it was Carrie who cared for him, the grandfather she had grown up believing to be her father.

Susan concluded in her survey that the population of Mingoose was mostly middle-aged and elderly. I checked again in 1985, by which time there were nineteen homes (the chapel had been converted and a chalet added to Mingoose Vale) with thirty-four inhabitants. Some of the dwellings had become holiday homes. The trend towards an ageing population, true of Cornwall as a whole, had continued. There were now twenty-six inhabitants over fifty, so that age group had doubled. No more children had been born or come into the hamlet.

What had happened to the seven children in Susan's survey? Sadly, two had died, a tragically high number for such a small place. Jimmy Pascoe died of cancer when he was twenty-one and David Murrish was killed in a car accident at the end of Scoll Lane. The others were up-country, in London or abroad, illustrating what is always said about young people in Cornwall: there are no

Milking time behind the barns of
Mingoose House

opportunities for them in the county and they are forced to leave home. Meanwhile the population grew older.

While growing older, the population of Mingoose became less Cornish. When we came here in 1961 the opposite side of the valley was completely Cornish. At Mingoose Farm were the Williams, who were a local family. Clifford Oates in the thatched cottage behind the chapel had been a miner. The chapel was still in use and was looked after by Carrie Yelland, who lived just down the road in the other thatched cottage with her son Martin. Old Mrs Pascoe lived in Mingoose House with her two daughters, Evelyn and Jean, and her son Jack lived in Ivy Cottage with his wife Mary and their boy Jimmy. Next down the hill was May Morrison in Mingoose Cottage. (She dropped 'Fanny' from her name in later life, but to her family she was always Fanny May.) The Waters lived at Briar Cottage.

Everyone on the northern side of the valley came from families which had been in the area for several generations, and many of them were inter-related. It was very much the traditional pattern. On the southern side of the valley the pattern had already been disrupted. Next to the stream, Wayside had been converted from a barn. A retired major lived there; he had come to the hamlet to breed mink, but had given it up and worked in the tax office in Truro. The 'mink house' stood for years under the pine trees, the most superior of the sheds scattered around Mingoose. His wife created a garden in which she worked every day, a radio on the ground beside her.

The artist Alec Wiles lived at Old Inn Cottage, which was then called Blue Gates. He was a portrait painter, cartoonist, sculptor - he could turn his hand to any form of art. As I went off to school in the morning I used to envy him. How marvellous to be a freelance, I thought. To stay at home and do what you wanted, when you wanted. That was the way to live.

There was a retired civil servant at Shasta, with his wife and sister-in-law, and the Murrishes at Fernbank. Ron Murrish was a quantity surveyor at County Hall. His great-great-grandfather was a miner who lived at Bolingey, in a valley leading to Perranporth. His life was described in The Miner of Perran-Zabuloe by the Reverend W. Davis Tyack. The book is a tribute to the friendship between the miner and the Methodist minister and I shall refer to it again later. There were Murrishes in Mingoose in the 1896 directory, and Irwin Murrish from Rose Cottage was Eddie Tredinnick's best friend.

The movement away from an indigenous population, working locally in the fields (like Jack Rashleigh) or in shops in St Agnes (like Evelyn Pascoe at the stores and Jean Pascoe at the Post Office) had started before we came to Mingoose Villa. Like the major, the artist and the retired civil servant, we were 'foreigners' or 'strangers'. I had been born in Somerset and Pep in Hampshire. I was a teacher who wanted to write and she was a nurse. I travelled the nine miles into Camborne each day; she looked after the children until they were all at school and she could go back to nursing. We never thought that we might be contributing to the decline of Cornish identity and the break-up of traditional rural patterns by living in Mingoose. It was all very simple. We liked the house, we liked the area and wanted to live here.

We never felt that we were outsiders. Quite the contrary, we were made very welcome. Most people were glad to see three more children in the hamlet, as even then there was the feeling that it was dying, a place for the elderly. Sunday School numbers at the chapel doubled at a stroke. If anyone felt that we were foreigners taking over a Cornish hamlet, they never expressed it. There is more awareness now of the effect over the years of people from away buying houses in Cornwall. Forty-five years ago there were no second homes or holiday lets.

The family before us at Mingoose Villa was even called

Jack Pascoe building a Cornish hedge at Mingoose Cottage

Evelyn and Jean Pascoe with Mary Morrison and children, haymaking in the paddock in front of Ivy Cottage

Audrey Winn at Floral Cottage,
converted into a single dwelling
by the nineteen-thirties

English. They had first seen the house before the war, when they were on holiday in Cornwall. They walked past and decided that one day they would buy it. Eventually the opportunity arose. Edwin Tredinnick said that for a while during the First World War a Spaniard lived here. He rented the house and received money from Spain every month; sometimes it was late. He walked around in a great black overcoat which reached to the ground and he wore nothing underneath. (How did Eddie know?) He had an English wife and they had a baby, born in the house. Once when the money didn't arrive, he burned whatever he could find inside, furniture and fittings. It must have been the Spaniard who pulled out all the dado rails in every room. You can see where they used to be, to protect the walls from chair backs, but there is only an uneven line of plaster now. When the money still didn't come, he went back to Spain and the owners found the house stripped bare. At about the same time D. H. Lawrence was in Cornwall, and the Spaniard sounds a Lawrentian character, trying to live a life free from the conventions of society.

Before that, in the nineteenth century, the house was leased by the church for thirty years, as the vicarage for Mount Hawke while the rectory there was being built. The vicars who lived here were Edward Montague Hamilton 1847-1862, Henry Stone 1862-1863, Henry Wheeler Brenton 1863-1868, William Avery 1868-1871, Isidore Daimpré 1871-1874 and William Henry Allin 1874-1879. (Sue did her homework thoroughly and I have copied her list.) John Dungay moved to the new vicarage in Mount Hawke. None of the names is particularly Cornish, especially Isidore Daimpré. He sounds pre-Raphaelite: I see him with long golden hair and mystical eyes, a Holman Hunt sort of clergyman. The only facts I know about him are that he took his degree at Trinity College, Dublin, and that his living was worth £125 a year.

The residents of Mingoose Villa have sometimes been 'foreigners', even literally. If we continue up the road to the Victory Inn the other four houses were lived in by Cornish families when we first came here. There was Audrey Winn at Floral Cottage, living alone after a brief marriage in the house where she was born and keeping a few bullocks in the fields on the side of the valley. She took in summer visitors in the traditional way. They had rooms in the house and provided the food which she cooked for them. One day she had a stroke and no one could get into the cottage; the police came and broke a window. When I came home Pep had moved her into our house, where she looked after her for three weeks until she died. An old Cornish couple lived at Tresco Farm, Mr and Mrs Hooper. They farmed in a very small way, milking a few cows. Then Mr Hooper died and Mrs Hooper sold up and moved.

It is not easy to define who is Cornish. You can join the political party Mebyon Kernow (The Sons of Cornwall) if you feel that you are Cornish, while the Cornish Nationalist Party expects you to have been born in Cornwall of Cornish parents. The Cornish Stannary Parliament defines as Cornish anyone who has at least one Cornish parent, and this has been my guide. Very often a husband or wife has come from out of the county. We have seen how Fanny May married William Morrison, a Scotsman from London. Janet Rashleigh married Fred Bawden, a Geordie from Tyneside despite his Cornish name, Jack Pascoe married Mary from South Wales.

In 1901 every household would have been Cornish by this definition. Sixty years later there were twelve out of eighteen. By 1985, with two more 'units of accommodation', there were nine out of twenty. In other words, over twenty-five years the Cornish population of Mingoose had declined from just over two-thirds to less than a half. By the end of the century it had dropped to five out of twenty-five, or just one fifth.

Fanny May's first child, Tim, on holiday at Mingoose House, c1920

Mingoose Cottage in the snow

Five more homes had been added, two barn conversions at the farm, a new farmhouse, a new house on Mr Martin's nursery and the restoration of the derelict cottage, making a total of twenty-five. Five of them were holiday lets or second homes. There were now forty-three inhabitants, ten of them children. As we move into the twenty-first century the hamlet seems to be more alive. People have arrived with families and although there is still a high proportion of retired people (eight households) the average age is less than it was at the low point of the mid-eighties.

As it becomes less Cornish, it has become more middle class. The value of property in Mingoose has increased so much that it is impossible for a young couple to live here, a story repeated throughout Cornwall. Three households are still connected with work on the land, but the major occupation now is not agriculture but medicine, with five doctors in the hamlet: it is an attractive area in which to live - 'much sought-after' in the words of the estate agents' adverts - and convenient for Treliske Hospital on the outskirts of Truro.

If James Tredinnick, miner and returned emigrant, butcher and farmer, Methodist and teetotaller, could come back a hundred years later he would recognise the landscape and the houses, but he would find the people very unfamiliar, even though he still has a great-grandson at Mingoose Cottage. He would find that his name has disappeared from the valley. The male line of the family continues only in the United States and apparently has little interest in its Cornish ancestry.

Roland Retallack

CHAPTER ELEVEN

The farm sale at Wheal Butson took place one day in the late summer of 1981. The farm is a mile or two from Mingoose by road but not far as the crow flies, just over the ridge by the old railway and into the next valley. It was a warm, bright day. There were cars parked in the shade beneath the hedge, all the way down the road to the bridge. The farm stood on a bend in the road on the hillside. It was black-roofed and white-walled, with grey stone and block outbuildings around it. Above and beyond, the slopes were covered with burrows, mine waste where nothing grew, and the fields were fawn-coloured after months without rain. There was not much water in the stream, or 'river' as Mr Retallack called it.

In the farmyard the auctioneers had chalked on walls and doors: CATTLE ... HAY ... 80 BALES STRAW. They had set a table and chairs inside the garage, facing the yard. The auction had brought out a lot of people, women in summer dresses and several old men, some of them quite small with shrivelled faces. They stood around in groups, chatting or moving slowly around looking at the piles of scrap metal, harness, tools, barrels and sacks. A group of women went from building to building, shaking their heads. "Oh, 'tis sad, the state of the place," they said. "Enough to keep anyone busy for ten years," remarked an old man in a straw hat. A few men in suits moved more purposefully than the rest. They had clip-boards in their hands and were from the firm of auctioneers.

Roland Retallack, a great-grandson of James Tredinnick, looked uncomfortably hot in a heavy pullover. He wore a farmer's cap and his trousers were tucked into his Wellington boots. The auctioneer took him into a quiet corner. Roland looked very determined, as though nothing would make him budge on his price.

A gate led out of the yard into a field, and there we waited. It was warm in the sun and everything seemed drowsy and timeless. Beyond the gate were the gentle slopes of the valley, the tawny fields and the low trees around the stream, where the banks were dried and brown. In the distance a combine harvester moved slowly across the hillside, its drone just audible.

The auctioneer stepped into the yard. He took his place behind the table, with Mr Retallack on one side and the solicitor and auctioneer's clerk on the other. He held out his arms like a preacher and invited everyone to come closer. He was a large, brown-suited man, full of bonhomie and confidence. He spoke of his old friend Roland Retallack and how sad it was that he had to give up farming because of his failing eyesight. But it was not an occasion for sentiment. "This is a real sale, ladies and gentlemen, and I'm sure Roland won't mind if I tell you that he's paid a deposit on a property in Mingoose. He wants to sell, and he's put a very realistic reserve on the farm." He introduced the solicitor who would read out the conditions of sale.

The solicitor's voice could not be heard and when he had finished the auctioneer sprang into action, making the most of the contrast between the dull reading of the legal conditions and the drama of the bidding. With a sense of urgency he tried to start at thirty-five thousand pounds. There were no takers, but someone offered twenty-five thousand. It quickly went up to thirty thousand, then moved slowly in increments of two hundred and fifty pounds.

There were interruptions from a man the auctioneer addressed as 'Cap'n'. The captain wanted to know the rateable value. Then he wanted to know if the farm was on the phone. The auctioneer said that it was all specified in the catalogue and would the Cap'n confine himself to genuine questions. He didn't interrupt any more.

The bidding approached thirty-five thousand pounds. A young man who had been persuaded to go up two hundred and fifty pounds a time shook his head. "At thirty-five thousand pounds then," said the auctioneer. "I offer it once, I offer it twice ... Gone!" He carried a broken-off cane and he brought it down with a great whack across the table. The farm was sold.

The buyer went forward to sign the contract. The audience seemed to breathe out and relax. They quickly passed round the name of the new owner, a pig-farmer who had sold his own farm and then was let down over the property he wanted. There would be no problem of ready money. Then another rumour went around, that he wasn't a pig-farmer at all, but a bank manager.

"Do 'ee pay VAT, boy?" the auctioneer shouted to Mr Retallack.

"I do pay," shouted Roland. "But I don't get it back."

There was sympathetic laughter from the crowd, as though he had made a good answer.

The auctioneer moved off around the yard, trying to take the crowd with him, though they now seemed inclined to break into smaller groups. He beat his cane against a galvanised water-tank, producing a hollow, drumming sound. He couldn't get a bid of five pounds for it. "Come on, ladies and gentlemen, I've seen people live in worse!" It went for two pounds. A pile of scrap metal sold for a pound. The next item was a barrel; he called for a hammer and chisel to break it open. It contained molasses and also made two pounds.

The chickens were sold for one pound and five pence each, and everyone moved towards the cattle shed. Interest, which had flagged during the selling of the small items, picked up again. A number of men pulled gates around the doorway to form a pen, with the wall of the building on one side and a stone hedge on the other. A tough, thick-set character in blue shirt and jeans broke open a bale of straw and scattered it on the ground. People sat on the hedge or leaned against the gates. The auctioneer entered the ring.

Roland was agitated. "They'll be frightened," he called, thinking of his cattle about to be driven into the pen. With his arms held out in front of him, for the sun was too bright for his eyes, he hurried to what he called the 'meat house', where he kept his corn.

He came back with a bowlful and tried to find a way into the pen, but there were too many people and he couldn't get through. When they saw what he wanted they stood back to make way. He went through the pen and into the barn, to feed and settle his animals.

The black and white cow came out first, pausing suspiciously at the door, surprised by the crowd staring at her. She put down her front legs and pulled her head back. "They're not used to people," called Roland from inside the barn. The thick-set man in blue patted her on the rump and kept her moving round and round, keeping her calm and remaining very phlegmatic himself.

The auctioneer praised the pregnant cow in glowing terms. He bent on his knees, looking at her from underneath and then from one side and the other. He made an estimate of her weight in which the upper and lower limits were so far apart that the audience laughed. The bidding was in guineas. There were three bidders, a youngish man in the doorway, a bald-headed man sitting on the hedge and a man in a pink shirt standing behind a gate. The cow went for four hundred and ninety guineas.

Next a cow and calf came into the ring, followed by the steers. They all made good prices. The auctioneer, a principal of the firm, had done his bit. He handed over to an assistant who would auction the furniture in front of the house. Purchasers settled their bills at the table in the garage and began loading their goods. A girl in a long Indian cotton dress cut her hand on the scrap metal she was carrying into a motorised caravan. The farmer who bought the chickens carried them by the legs and threw them into the back of a blue Morris van. The same man had bought one of the cows, but he couldn't pick her up until the next day.

"That's all right, boy," said Mr Retallack. "I'll let her out into the field, she could do with a feed. An' I'll milk her in the morning. Leave her a week if you like!"

Cattle trucks backed up to the barn and people carried furniture out of the house. An elderly woman was delighted with a picture she had bought, a print of a fair-haired girl in an Alice-like dress, embracing a St Bernard dog beneath a bough of mistletoe. "It's some lovely," she kept saying, showing it to everyone. It had perhaps belonged to Roland's grandmother, the sentimental and tragic Winnie Rickard. Two young men carried off an enormous trunk.

John Pearce, butcher, of Trane Farm
Mingoose, outside St Agnes vicarage
in the late nineteenth century

The furniture was sold and the crowd was dispersing. The only people left inside were trying to bring a wardrobe down from a bedroom, but it was wedged firmly on the stairs. It had been bought by a woman in orange trousers. She hinted in her north-country accent that she ought to have her money back, but the auctioneers had packed up and gone. Some helpers took the sashes out of one of the bedroom windows and lowered the wardrobe on a rope. Through the open space could be seen a brown field in the slight dip of the valley, and one brown and white cow in the middle. It all seemed very peaceful.

But Mr Retallack, left alone in the house with just his bed, a table and a chair, was unable to sleep. The cow had been separated from her calf and she was "hootin', hootin', hootin' " all night.

At the end of the month on the quarter day he arrived in Mingoose, perched on the back of a tractor driven by a neighbouring farmer. Behind it was a trailer laden with bits of furniture, bales of straw, pieces of wood and sheets of galvanised iron. I helped them to unload as they were blocking the road. "Clearing out?" asked Mr Williams as he waited in his car to pass by. "Moving in," I said. The farmhouse table went through the door, but only just.

As a boy, Roland used to visit his Aunt May at Mingoose Cottage. His family was not well-off, though they never went, as he said, 'bootless'. His aunt May was very good to them. His father Jack Retallack had married May's eldest sister Winnie (Carrie's

Theresa Rickard, Roland's mother,
at Rickard's Tea Rooms,
Chapel Porth, c1910

mother) when she became a widow after Edward's death in South Africa. Winnie had a daughter by Jack, but died in 1913 when she was only thirty-nine. Jack then married Theresa, the eldest of her four daughters by Edward Rickard. At the time it was perfectly legal, though it caused consternation in the village and the chapel. A deputation of elders called to inspect the marriage certificate.

Theresa Arminda (Winnie had been imaginative in the naming of her daughters) was Roland's mother. They lived at Carn Bargus, and later at Wheal Butson. Roland always stayed at home working on the farm. His father gave him sixpence a week pocket money, on the understanding that one day the farm would be his. Coulter Hancock (Junior) met Jack at the cattle market one day and insisted that he came to his office to make the arrangement legal. When he was twenty-seven Roland began to suffer from a raging thirst as he worked in the fields. He went to the doctor, who sent him to the City Hospital in Truro. He was diagnosed as diabetic and had to start giving himself a daily injection of insulin. By about this time he had saved nine pounds, all in sixpenny pieces.

His father became ill and took to his bed. Roland carried up his meals and spent every evening sitting with him, though his father had always been hard on him. He had tried once to make him kill a pig. He had always killed his own pigs, he'd chase a pig across a field until it dropped (a pig always gives in) and then he'd knife it. Roland couldn't kill a pig. "I ken't do it, feyther," he said. "No such word as ken't," said his father, holding down the pig and making him take the knife. "Stick it in, boy." But Roland couldn't do it.

He listened to his father night after night for six weeks. One evening his father said, "Hold my hand, boy, and see me out proper." Roland held his hand and five minutes later the old man died.

Roland stayed on in the house with his mother, until she too became ill and went to live with a relative. When she died, no one thought to tell him. He heard from the butcher on the day of the funeral. He lived alone at the farm. His sight was failing, but he continued to work. It became more and more difficult, and he sold off thirty acres and most of his herd of cows. He struggled on for another year or two, until he realised that he had to sell up and move.

It took him a while to get used to Shasta Cottage. It had been a holiday let, with fitted carpets in every room and a lot of rather

Joe Yelland senior, Martin's grandfather and son-in-law of John Pearce;
he lived at Chapel Villa in the early
years of the twentieth century

dainty furniture. "I don't know what my mother would have said about it," he exclaimed, amused at the thought. And then, changing his tone, he added, "I know what feyther would have said. 'You don't want all this, boy - get rid of it!' "

At first he was very restless. All his life he had worked seven days a week, through all the hours of daylight. He had never done anything else, except join the Home Guard during the war. It was very difficult to stop working and the first day he 'teeled' a patch of ground to plant the rhubarb crowns he had brought from Wheal Butson. He was always looking for a job to keep him busy. He helped fell the elm trees and clear the entrance to the field opposite Mingoose Villa. It was a damp, shady spot. "This ground is gifted with ivy," he said. Every ground had its own gift; some was gifted with charlock, some with nettles, some with 'disels'. It could also be gifted with diseases; Mrs Winn's ground was gifted with redwater, somebody else's with lumpy-jaw. 'Disels' were thistles, sow disels and Scotch disels, and foxgloves were 'poppies' because they could be popped. Poppies were 'corn roses', daffodils were 'Lent lilies' and buttercups were 'kingcups'.

After six months he no longer wanted to be sawing wood or doing something active all the time. He kept a few chickens in the garden, in a wooden hut on wheels beneath the apple trees. The birds were Rhode Island cross, light brown in colour and white underneath if their feathers were ruffled. They scratched with one foot, scratched with the other, moved back and pecked. They made sudden rushes, their stubby wings flapping and seemed unable to brake, bumping into one another. They laid well, and Mr Retallack and Mrs Rashleigh between them kept Mingoose self-sufficient in eggs.

Some people didn't think he was blind, as they saw him marching down Scoll Lane to catch the bus to Truro on market day. He could see a little out of the sides of his eyes, and some days were better than others. He was not much good on very bright days or very misty days. On other occasions he could just about make out where he was and where he was going. Later, like his great-grandfather, he lost his sight totally.

He liked to gossip about people he used to know. If any calamity befell them, it made them all the more interesting. He knew a man once who coughed up his lung. "What right up?" "Yes, he brought it right up. A good job it was his right lung." "Why?" "Because if it was his left lung he would have died." "What a load of rubbish you talk, Roland!" said Pep.

When he talked about the farm, it was a catalogue of disasters. There was a cow that had a calf and the afterbirth didn't come away. It came away later in the meadow and her womb with it. The vet pushed it back and sewed her up. Roland stayed with her in the field all night, to keep her standing still and give the womb a better chance of bedding down. She recovered, but she was always a bad-tempered cow after that. She slapped him across the eye once with her tail, and he believed that was what brought on his blindness.

Another cow ate the afterbirth that had been dropped in the meadow and choked to death. He took the body to the knackers. "I couldn't work there," he said, "'tis hell on earth. But the men there think nawthing of it. They'll kill a bullock and sit down on top of 'un to eat their pasty."

He had two horses, Prince and Madam. His father sold Prince for ten pounds when he was a year old and bought him back for twenty pounds a year later. Prince was never properly broken, so he always had to be tied back. He once bolted with the 'osso'.

"What's an 'osso'?"

He exaggerated the 'h' sounds. "The horse hoe," he said, sounding very posh.

His father was knocked to the ground and the blade of the hoe took off his hat. If it had touched his head it would have finished him. Prince ended up in the hedge, with one shaft broken. They sold him later for thirty-three pounds. The secret of breaking in a horse is to use a night halter. Some people try to do it with 'mops up', but that's no good, the horse must see everything. 'Mops' are blinkers.

There was nothing like his mother's cooking. It was poor man's food, rough but good. She'd take a turnip from the fields, 'moor' it (clean it) and boil it. Or she'd take a flatpole, a cow cabbage, and make it into a broth, with some suet, butcher's suet, not these white chopped-up little bits that you get nowadays, and some currants to sweeten it. If the cats brought in any rabbits, she'd grab them and put them into a stew. She made a lovely tatie cake.

He believed that there was no freedom any longer. You used to be able to do what you liked with your own land, but now they won't let you. The aim of the National Trust is to take your land from you. Councillors are out for their own interests. They get paid fifteen pounds a meeting; if they go to three an evening, it adds up. Freemasons look after their own; if they commit a crime they always get away with it. They control the courts and you never want to get on the wrong side of a Freemason. He knew one who was caught red-handed, stealing chickens. He was sent to Bodmin and he walked in the door and straight out again. That was all that happened to him.

But Jimmy went to prison for six months during the war. When he came out he was starving. He said he'd been glad to eat

A flock of sheep on Mingoose Hill

Jean Pascoe with goat and kids in the paddock of Mingoose House

raw potato-peelings. People made a collection for him and gave him a great reception. They missed the meat that he had supplied them with. He bought a pig from Roland's father once. He left his van some way away and walked down the road in the dark. "I haven't got my humane killer with me today, Jack," he said. He never had his humane killer, he never used one. He took a hammer and hammered the old sow, but she wouldn't go down. Roland couldn't stand it. He went back to the house. "There's agony going on down there," he told his mother. "Agony!"

Jimmy took something with a point to it and the old sow scat down like a jacket. He split her in half and weighed one side only, the small side so that he wouldn't pay the full value. A neighbour came down the next day and saw the cauldron for boiling water. "You feeding your bullocks hot mash then, Jack?" he asked knowingly.

When it was drizzling outside, it was 'skiffing' or 'skiffy'. It was not good weather for his eyes and he sat indoors, listening for the clock to strike. He couldn't see the hands or 'flies'. At Christmas he liked to eat 'pasty-nuts', which he scat open on the hearth amongst the ashes and 'churks'. "Jesus Whizzigans, as my old feyther used to say," he would exclaim, as he missed the Brazil and hit his thumb. Sometimes he didn't shave for a few days, but he didn't want anyone to think he was looking as rough as rats. Bullfinches were as wild as hermits. A certain woman smoked like a tar barrel and another drank like a launder. He preserved the ways of speech of the countryside of a century earlier, uninfluenced by modern idioms. It was a language which served his purpose and he used it unselfconsciously.

Time seemed to pass very slowly for him. He spent hours sitting alone in his cottage, waiting for the 'flies' of the clock to reach the hour. His life had been the farm.

Public Houses and Summer Visitors

CHAPTER TWELVE

Isaac John Richards was the son of a well-to-do farmer at Lanner Barton, St Allen, near Truro. The two boys, Isaac and Albert, went to Truro School when it first opened, riding in daily and stabling their horses. But I.J., as he was always known, even to his wife, did not like farming and when he inherited the barton he sold up and moved to Lamorna at Towan Cross and then to Mingoose Villa.

What he enjoyed was an audience. He would stroll to the front gate, the wrought-iron gate with spikes and curlicues that still hangs between granite posts. In front of it is a small triangle of ground with the road dropping away below, forming a natural pulpit. Here he would stand smoking his pipe and in no time at all he had gathered a group of men around him. I cannot imagine where they came from.

Although he only stayed a short while - he inherited a property in Truro - he made several changes to the house. He removed the arched window on the stairs and added in 1938 the extension for bathroom above and scullery below. There was already indoor sanitation in Mingoose, at Eddie Tredinnick's Californian-inspired Fernbank, but it was still new enough for all the neighbours to come and see. Mrs Richards complained of them 'traipsing over her canvas' (linoleum). He knocked down the old privy, (digging out the foundations for a boiler house, I discovered a circular chamber a metre deep cut in the solid rock and filled with very fine black soil) and had a Cornish pit constructed by the gate. It is very deep, lined with squared stone, and has only been emptied once when it filled with tree roots.

I.J.'s daughter Joy Stevenson, the dialect recorder for the Old Cornwall Society, came to visit us after a chance encounter. It was the first time she had returned to the house since leaving it as a child. When they lived at Towan Cross, she used to come and play with the Coleman children who then lived here and who were allowed to run wild. They roamed barefoot through the valley and over the downs, where they kept goats. Betty Tredinnick knew them when she lived next door at Fernbank. They were educated

Goats on the downs, c1930

at home and had a private tutor who came over from Rosemundy in St Agnes. Miss Roosmale-Cocq - a name you couldn't make up - was a clergyman's daughter who had grown up in the West Indies. Betty joined them for lessons when she was four years old and it was in our sitting room that she learned to read. It would be interesting to know more of the Colemans, this rather hippy family ahead of their time.

Joy loved playing with the children because of their freedom. They made a den in the dark cupboard under the stairs between the kitchen and the dairy, where they lit candles. When she moved into the house she thought that she would continue to use it as a den for herself and her brother, to play in by candlelight. But her mother was horrified at the idea of candles under the stairs and soon put a stop to their game.

The Richards had a live-in maid, a girl of about sixteen called Doris. She had bright red hair and slept downstairs, in the back kitchen or dairy. If she was going to St Agnes for the evening, to a chapel meeting or the Regal cinema, I.J. would say to her, "Mind how you go, Doris. Take care of your saffron bun!" Joy couldn't understand why Doris blushed so.

In the local dialect 'to go up lappy-side' was to go to the Victory Inn, presumably to lap or sup a pint. I.J. loved to go up lappy-side. He had his own chair from where he held court. To the despair of his wife, he was very generous and was always buying rounds of drinks. As a result he was extremely popular and never short of people to listen to him. The landlord at the time was Charles

Towan Cross looking towards the Victory Inn, c1905

Found. He was very keen on wrestling, organising taxi parties to go to matches. For a week afterwards he would remain very excited, grabbing people in the bar to demonstrate the holds. I.J. said that he had 'hands like shovels'.

Another regular at the Victory Inn was 'Sunshine' Curtis. He was a miner who had been injured in an explosion, leaving him disfigured. He could only do light work and visitors, feeling sorry for him, would often buy him a drink. One visitor bought him a pint of beer and was amazed at the speed with which it disappeared. "You drank that quickly," he said, thinking his evening would be expensive at that rate. "I don't take any risks," said Sunshine. "I had a glass knocked over once." The story was recounted by Ernie Landry.

A photograph taken before the First World War shows three cloth-capped men standing outside the inn, one holding a bicycle. Apart from the addition of a porch, the inn has changed little. A board over the door says:

THE VICTORY INN

BY

H.F. DUCKHAM

LICENSED TO BREW BEER

RETAILER OF

WINES, SPRITS, TOBACCO

In the right-hand side window is an advertisement for OXO,

The Victory Inn, c1905

Old Inn Cottge and Shasta in the snow

which was sold at tuppence a cup.

The Victory Inn was not always the only public house in the area. Old Inn Cottage lies just off the road near the stream in the bottom of the valley. In the nineteenth century it was The Miners' Arms. A sale advertisement in the West Briton of the 17th February 1826 offered a 'Public House at Mingues, now in occupation of Mr John Julian. Premises within three-quarter mile of Great Wheal Towan, South Towan, Wh. Charlotte and several other mines in full work. There is a fine stream of water that runs within 10 yeards (sic) of the House.' Evidently what mattered to a pub in those days was to be close to a good supply of water and of miners. The same John Julian is recorded twelve years earlier, in 1814, as the tenant of Tregeas Vicarage House, near the Church Town in St Agnes, 'now and for many years past used and much frequented as a Public House.' He must have moved 'over to Mingoose', as the St Agnes people have always said.

The publican of The Miners' Arms whose name was given to Sue when she wrote her project was Alexander Stephens. His name appears in Kelly's Directory for 1856 as 'Stephens Alexander, Miners' Arms and rate collector, Mingoose.' He is still there in 1873, though he is no longer collecting rates. Alexander Stephens brewed his own beer in what is now Shasta Cottage. When James Tredinnick's father William, who was born in 1819, was a boy he used to be paid a penny to read the West Briton to the miners in the evening. The room that became Val Maltwood's sitting room was reserved for the mine managers and their captains. They would meet there to discuss business and plan their operations, sitting over a jug of ale; they liked it mulled, with sugar. They had a slate in front of the fire, on which was drawn a map of the shafts and levels of the mines.

There were once three ale-houses in Mingoose. The Victory Inn was the oldest-established and the only proper tavern, in that it could provide food and accommodation. The kidley-wink at Mingoose Villa probably opened soon after 1830, when the 'Beer Bill' removed the tax on beer and cider and made it possible for any rate-payer to obtain a licence from the excise officer on payment of two guineas. There was an immediate spate of new drinking houses and John Julian moved up the road from The Miners' Arms and went into business at our house, for the Tithe Survey of 1841 lists him as occupier of the tenement, garden and field.

There was probably too much competition. The peak years for the number of licensed premises in the country as a whole were in the eighteen-thirties. We know that by 1846 the house was available to rent and as beer-houses were considered places of low repute, it is hardly likely that it passed straight from kidley-wink to vicarage. I imagine that it went out of business very soon after 1841 about the same time as many other beer-houses, their keepers either bankrupted by giving too much credit or disillusioned by the lack of trade.

The Miners' Arms by the ford across the stream closed before the end of the century. The number of licensed premises had been declining throughout the period. The power to grant licences had been taken away from the Excise and given to the magistrates, who often refused to renew them especially if there were reports of drunkenness. The temperance movement, too, had had considerable success. Meetings were held in towns and villages all over Cornwall, including St Agnes, and many like James Tredinnick came forward to sign the pledge of total abstinence.

The decline in the population finally ensured the closure of Alexander Stephens's business. Sue was told it closed in 1899 but it must have been earlier. The Miners' Arms had dropped out of the directory by 1883, and it probably ceased to be an inn around about 1880. The mines were closing and the miners emigrating, and as the advertisement of 1826 showed, they had always been

Alexander Stephens on his horse outside the former Miners' Arms; Edith Murrish holds the children and Hilda Murrish leans against the hedge, c1905

the main customers. There were fewer people in Mingoose and those that remained were drinking less. The hamlet which had supported three licensed premises in the eighteen-thirties could now support no more than one. Edwin Tredinnick remembered seeing all the pub benches and trestles piled in Shasta Cottage.

According to local tradition, this was when the Victory Inn gained its name. It had defeated its two rivals. It was run at this time by two sisters, Nanny and Jean Argall. When Susan researched her project, Carrie Yelland told her that she used to fetch 'barm', deposited after the beer was made, from the Argalls' to make barm cake. I heard the story of the victorious Argalls several times, and in some versions there was a wager over which public house would survive. In Old Cornish Inns, H. L. Douch wrote that there were seven Victory Inns which exist or have existed in Cornwall, and that they were named after Nelson's flagship at the Battle of Trafalgar, 1805. So which is correct, historical research or oral tradition? As the pub by the stream closed in the eighties, any earlier use of the name Victory Inn would disprove the story. In Kelly's Directory of 1856, the first of the commercial addresses is 'Argall, Wm Hy Victory, Towan Cross'. Further down the list is 'Stephens Alexander, Miners' Arms'. In 1873 they are again both listed, though the licensee of the Victory Inn is now 'Argall Elizabeth (Miss)'. I assume that she was the daughter of William Henry, the 'Nanny' remembered by Carrie Yelland and sister to Jean. But if both names were in use at the same time, from the fifties to the seventies, the 'Victory' could not refer to the defeat of The Miners' Arms. Perhaps it had always been a boast of the Argalls, that with their name they would win in the end. Perhaps their survival at the expense of the other two gave rise to a joke explanation and the story came to be taken as true. Oral history is often unreliable, but true or false, such stories are part of the history of a place.

When we moved into our house, we found in an outbuilding, on a ledge between the top of the wall and the scantle slate roof, a worm-eaten old sign. It had ACCOMMODATION written on it in curly lettering. It probably dated from the nineteen-twenties. It would have been more exciting if it had been the original licensing board displayed over the door, with the name of John Julian. As the title deeds date only from the end of the century, we have no records of those early years. Kelly's Directory of 1897 has 'Richards William Henry, auctioneer and valuer' at Mingoose Villa. (He was no relation to the later I.J. Richards.) There is an Alex Stephens, farmer, at Towan Cross, and Miss Elizabeth Argall is at the Victory Inn. To come across her name for the first time in print was like navigating at sea and finding the landfall come up over the horizon in the expected place.

The board showed that our house had taken in visitors - the 'summer folk' - in the years between the wars. There is a postcard of the house by Hawke of Helston from about this time. It is in black and white, and has a number, 474, and the name Mingoose Villa written in white ink across the shade in the bottom right-hand corner. It is a very idyllic image. The trees are bare, but the sun is bright and the shadows strong. The front of the house is covered with ivy, cut square at the windows. The windows themselves have the original sixteen-pane sashes and the roof has the original slates, with a few patches here and there. The lane, the path to the front gate between the granite posts and the road sweeping round the corner are neatly sanded and gravelled. The house has never looked better.

The card was on sale to visitors. They stayed with Mrs Oram and later with Mrs Webb. Jane Webb told Eddie Tredinnick that she had been one of the bal-maidens who worked in the valley. (Three hundred, she said, but that sounds like an exaggeration.) She must have found taking in summer visitors much easier. They have stayed over the years in most of the houses of Mingoose;

only two or three have never had a spell as second home, holiday let or bed and breakfast establishment. In the seventies Old Inn Cottage was run as a guest house by Richard and Johnny, who was Polish and who had lived through the Warsaw uprising of 1944. They gave it its name and put up an inn-type sign on a post. Before that it had been Blue Gates and before that Shasta Villa. Shasta Cottage was part of the guest house, as it had been when it was an inn.

We joined the bed and breakfast trade in our early days here. We charged ten shillings a night at first, though fifteen shillings was the price for several years. I think it went up to a pound and even thirty shillings before Pep returned to work as a district nurse. The season was short. There were just two weeks of the summer, the first two of August, when Cornwall was bursting at the seams and people were desperate to find accommodation. They enquired from house to house or were directed by people who had heard you might have a spare room.

Early one evening I heard a car screech to a halt outside the back door. I went out and the driver said, in a strong Irish accent, "Have you got any accommodation?"

"Yes," I said. The house was empty.

"I'll take it," he said.

"Wouldn't you like to see the room?"

"No, that's all right."

"Perhaps your wife would like to see it?" I asked, vaguely aware of a figure alongside him in the car.

"She won't mind," he said. "We'll go for a meal and be back later."

He reversed the car, a bright red car with a hire-agency sign in the window. He went fast down the drive, scraping the sides and knocking some stones out of the bank. He hadn't even asked the price.

They returned at eight o'clock. The car roared up to the back door and they came in to the kitchen. Pep had come home and we made introductions.

"You can call me Paddy Murphy," he said, not even trying to make it sound like his real name. He was about forty years old, with a round face and freckles and ginger hair. He looked like a stage Irishman.

Mingoose Villa, photographed by Hawke of Helston in the nineteen-twenties

But his wife was even more incredible. "This is Inge," he said. She had blonde hair and was in her early twenties; she looked like a film star or model.

We offered them a drink and they tried to converse together. But it seemed that she couldn't understand a word of English and he couldn't understand a word of German. We did our best to interpret for them. Inge went to bed and Paddy stayed for a glass of beer.

Naturally the conversation turned to Ireland. It was in the early days of violence and I made what I thought was a fairly innocuous remark, about how the activities of the IRA had forfeited any sympathy I had once had for the republican cause.

The effect upon Paddy Murphy was startling. He turned red and clenched his fists. He delivered a speech about why the British Army should get out of Ireland and listed all the atrocities that the army had committed. It was impossible to get in a word. He finished his beer and went to bed.

They stayed for three days and the pattern of each day was the same. Paddy wanted an early breakfast, after which he left immediately in the car. Inge had no breakfast and stayed in bed all day, reading. She had a stack of novels by Heinrich Böll. Paddy came back at five o'clock every day, they went out for a meal and went straight to bed when they came in.

On the third day he came back in the morning, when I was at school. He told Pep that they were leaving and he wanted to settle the bill, only he had no cash until he'd been to the bank in Truro. They'd be back later; meanwhile he'd left their luggage in the hall.

I came home. They hadn't returned and we wondered if we would ever see them again. We went to look at the luggage. It was in the hall behind the inner door, where you couldn't see it from inside the house. It consisted of one case. It was so battered and ancient that it looked as though it had been picked off a dump. That's the last we see of Paddy Murphy, we thought. The case probably contained old newspapers or rocks.

And then we looked at each other and at the case again. It had gradually dawned on us. It might be a bomb ... I listened. It wasn't ticking, but do bombs necessarily tick? We didn't know.

I think that later if a man with an Irish accent, a self-declared supporter of the IRA, left a case in your house and made off fast, you wouldn't hesitate. You'd call the police. But at that time there hadn't been any bombings on the mainland, only in Northern Ireland. We just couldn't believe it. Why pick on Cornwall? Why us? We weren't important enough. We'd feel too stupid, ringing the police to say we had reason to believe that the IRA had planted a bomb in our house. In Mingoose? They'd only laugh.

We decided to give them until seven o'clock. At about twenty to seven the red car came rocketing up the drive. Paddy Murphy leapt out and took a wad of notes from his pocket. He peeled off nine of them and then reached inside the car. Inge passed him a large, flat packet. "We'd like you to accept this little token of our appreciation for all you have done for us," he said. It sounded like a citation for gallantry, a reward for services to the Irish Republican Army.

It looked like a record. We took off the wrapping, wondering what they had chosen. It was Jacqueline du Pré, playing Haydn's cello concerto in C and Boccherini's cello concerto in B flat. Paddy fetched the case, slammed it in the boot, and backed down the drive at full speed, bumping from side to side and knocking out a few more stones.

We went inside and played the disc. It was perfect.

The Life of a Miner

CHAPTER THIRTEEN

It would have been too much like fiction if our bed and breakfast guests had been terrorists. But there was something very suspect about Paddy Murphy. Even if he wasn't a terrorist, was he really some sort of agent? There are plenty of reasons why he would have come to Cornwall. He could have been trying to make contact with the extremists in the Cornish nationalist movement, though I don't think he would have found many. He could have been reconnoitring the Ministry of Defence establishment at Nancekuke, at that time producing the CS gas that was being used in Northern Ireland. He might have been setting up a supply line for the running of guns.

There are traditional links between Cornwall and Southern Ireland. It hadn't all been a one-way traffic of empty beer barrels and Irish saints like St Piran, the patron saint of tinners, who sailed from Ireland on a millstone (a coracle, perhaps?) and landed at Perranporth. In the second half of the eighteenth century and early in the nineteenth a lot of contraband cargo was trans-shipped to Ireland, and the north coast of Cornwall was as busy as the south. Irish ships sailed into Newquay and Padstow to load smuggled cargoes brought overland from the south coast. Perhaps Paddy Murphy wanted to find out whether he could re-establish the old routes into Southern Ireland.

In the eighteenth century the Cornish miner was regarded as a terrorist by the authorities, who constantly feared insurrection and stationed soldiers in the main towns. There were many riots and disturbances, usually caused by the impossibility of feeding a family on the low wages. When corn was scarce and prices rose, the tinner could not afford to buy. His resentment was increased by seeing it exported from Cornish ports to sell overseas. He resorted to desperate measures and hardly a winter passed without groups of miners breaking into cellars, barns or ships' holds to carry off quantities of corn.

At the beginning of 1757 several hundred tinners assembled in St Agnes; they must have included some from Mingoose. (There were a number of small, separate workings in the area and the

The workforce at Towanroath shaft, Wheal Coates, early in the twentieth century

mines which became known later as Wheal Towan were already active, producing nine tons of copper ore in the same year.) The intention of the miners was to march on Padstow and seize what corn they could find. They sent an advance party of ten men, who reported that there was barley in the town and that the inhabitants would put up no resistance. Late in the afternoon, the St Agnes men with several women and a hundred horses entered Padstow. They immediately began to break open warehouses and load their horses with corn. They sold or gave away what they could not carry. At the quay was a sloop bound for Guinea and they tried to board her, thinking she carried a cargo of grain. The captain fired some blank shot and then let two men come on board to see for themselves that there was no corn in the vessel. The miners stayed in the town all night, 'huzzaing and carousing', and the last did not leave until ten o'clock the next morning. It was two or three days before a party of soldiers marched into the town.

The miners were able to overawe the farmers in the market towns, often fixing their own prices. At Truro market one Wednesday in August 1766 the farmers were charging twenty-one shillings per Cornish bushel for wheat. A party of tinners assembled and the farmers were obliged to let them have wheat at fourteen shillings a bushel. On the following Friday the tinners went into Redruth and forced the farmers there to sell at the same price as in

98

Truro, with butter at sixpence per pound and potatoes at tuppence-halfpenny per gallon.

In 1773 they were back again in Padstow, this time with seven or eight hundred men. They offered seventeen shillings for corn, and when they were refused they broke open doors and took it for nothing. There were eighteen soldiers by now to protect the town, but the miners rushed them and wrested the firelocks out of their hands. They went on to Wadebridge, where they found more corn stored for export, and this they also carried away. The Padstow riots spread and for ten days the tinners roamed the high roads, plundering farmhouses and malthouses and knocking down anyone who opposed them. There was a skirmish between a party of miners and the soldiers quartered at Pendennis Castle: a tinner and a woman were shot dead.

In the last years of the eighteenth century the tin industry was in decline. It was impossible for the miners to emigrate, the solution to the depression of a hundred years later. They could only work for next to nothing or roam the countryside plundering and stealing. If a ship was wrecked on the coast, it is not surprising that they would strip it within twelve hours, between the tides.

The condition of these wild and desperate men, regarded as savages by the rest of society, changed dramatically in the next fifty years. The miner had been the terror of eighteenth-century Cornwall; within a single generation there were amongst them men of education and culture. The change was due partly to the revival in the fortunes of the tin industry in the early nineteenth century. Scores of new mines were started. The shaft in our garden was sunk in 1809. Wheal Towan reopened, and where it had produced nine tons of copper ore in the year of the Padstow Riots, it produced nearly nine thousand tons within the next four years. As a result, the population increased and many cottages in Mingoose date from this period, including most of those that were lived in for a hundred years and then allowed to decay. The introduction of steam and machinery made it possible to mine to a greater depth and therefore more profitably, and made slightly less intolerable the labour of the miner. He no longer had to pump and winch by hand, and the invention of the 'man-engine' enabled him to ride to the surface at the end of his 'core', instead of climbing by ladders. The system of wages, by which a miner made his own contract to work a particular

Briar Cottages, once a row of miners' cottages

Carrie and Joe Yelland with Martin,
feeding the chickens

pitch, meant that he was almost his own master. With the exercise of skill and judgement, he earned enough to live on. He was better off than his counterpart in the coalmines or an agricultural labourer, and once or twice in his working life, if he struck lucky, he could expect to earn as much as fifty pounds in a month. This would enable him to buy the lease on a piece of land for the length of three lives and build himself a house; he could keep a pig and a cow or two. He worked shorter hours than most nineteenth-century industrial workers. The day was divided into three eight-hour 'cores' or shifts - sometimes four of six hours - and this gave him time to spend on his other interests. As described by Martin Yelland, it seemed an almost idyllic way of life, eight hours in the mine and eight on his smallholding, which produced enough food for him and his family to live well.

It could never have been quite as perfect as this and for many miners it was still a life of poverty, hardship and disease, as A.K. Hamilton Jenkin shows in The Cornish Miner. But clearly the old men that Martin Yelland knew recalled it as a good way of life. No doubt they were more fortunate than others, each having his own cottage and a few fields. The fields of Mingoose still have their nineteenth-century pattern: long narrow strips in the bottom of the valley, and steep patches of land on the hillsides. They are all small, with their original hedges and small sheds. On the flat uplands between the valleys the hedges have been removed to make large units suitable for farm machinery.

When we first came here, Sam Waters still dug one of the fields behind Briar Cottages by hand, to grow early potatoes and lettuces. At the turn of the century Tom Langdon lived there. He was a master mason, a 'bossman' at Wheal Kitty mine in St Agnes, and he cultivated the three or four small fields attached to the cottage. When Joe Yelland, the father of Martin, left school he went to work at the tin-streaming in Jericho valley, until he was old enough to go down the mines. He went to the United States for three or four years and when he came back before the First World War he rented Rose Cottage. It, too, had a few fields and he kept poultry, ran an egg collecting and packing business and worked in the mines. This way of life, combining mining and smallholding, continued into the twentieth century. As a young man, Roland Retallack of Shasta Cottage worked on his father's farm while his

Martin with his bicycle

father worked in the mines, right up to the Second World War.

The other great influence which changed the life of the miner in the nineteenth century was the Methodist movement. The Reverend W. Davis Tyack was appointed to the St Agnes circuit in 1850 to be one of two ministers and in his book The Miner of Perran-Zabuloe or Simple Records of a Good Man's Life, published in 1867, he recalled his first visit to Bolingey chapel near Perranporth, where all was 'orderly, fresh and cheerful, and the congregation - chiefly miners, their wives and families - were well-dressed, their boots and shoes blacked and shining.' The principal men of the society sat near the pulpit and led the singing. Amongst them was William Murrish, 'with massive forehead, soft, hazel, intelligent eyes, and - miner though he was, - fresh and ruddy countenance. A man of middle height - strongly built - presenting in face and form an embodiment of quiet power. He had a fine, mellow voice, and sang well.'

Joe Yelland rebuilding the chimney of Rose Cottage

At the end of the service, the friends came forward to welcome the new preacher and accompany him down the hill and through the valley. Later he frequently visited William Murrish's cottage and saw him surrounded by his family. 'And the many conversations with him, as he accompanied me part of the way home, after evening services, and rambles by the sea, revealed to me a depth of piety - a soundness of judgement - a refinement of taste - an amount of common sense, and of general intelligence; together with such humility, simplicity and cheerfulness, and affection, as combined to make his friendship a privilege of no common order.'

William Murrish was the great-great-grandfather of our neighbour at Fernbank and Ron Murrish was born in the cottage on Cox Hill that Davis Tyack had visited. At the minister's request, William Murrish wrote a sketch of his own life. He was born in 1818, the fifth of eleven children. When he was four, his father built a house at Reen Common, to be nearer the mine where he worked and to have a quieter place in which to bring up his family. They were all musical and frequently struck up a tune in the evenings. 'My brother James sang bass; Martin, the air; my sisters, Nancy and Sally, first and second treble; father and mother, who had both been church singers in their day, would also join; and all the rest, from myself down to the youngest that could speak - making a most delightful harmony.'

Ron Murrish taking his daughter
Elaine to her wedding

William had nine months' schooling, but it was his mother who taught him to read. 'After that I needed no one to stimulate me. I read then for the love I had of it.' He read the Bible when he was six and used to spend several hours together 'in perusing an old thick volume, without any covers, on geography' and two old volumes of the Methodist Magazine. The family took several magazines, Youth's Instructions, The Child's Magazine and The Child's Companion. He began to form a library for himself.

When he was twelve years old, his brother Martin died; it made a great impression on his mind. There was a religious revival in the neighbourhood about the same time and he and his sisters joined the class-meeting, though he was in doubts and fears. His father was injured when working underground and had his right leg amputated. Under the power of the 'Curse of Britain' - drink - his father lost his faith and gave up his connection with the church. William, too, stopped going to the class-meeting. He went to public houses and beer shops and being connected with singers, often stayed too long. Perhaps he came to our house, sang in our kitchen.

His father had been ailing for some months. On his way home from Summercourt Fair, where he had sold a cow and bought a pony, he attempted to climb on its back and in doing so broke a blood vessel. He only lived six hours. His mother died within the short space of sixteen days and there were seven children left at home without a father or mother. William and his sister Nancy took charge of the family. It laid a weight of care and thought upon him, which helped, he thought, to bring about his conversion.

In 1840, at the age of twenty-two, he began to correspond with his cousin William Kernick, seeking jointly to improve their education. He wrote first about music and teetotalism, but his cousin replied that another subject had arrested his attention for some time, and that subject was religion. This surprised him, as it had occupied his own thoughts in the months before, though he had kept it to himself. They both began to pray and one Sunday, with another young friend, they went to Perranwell chapel. 'There were tears of joy shed in the class that morning, by the leader and the old members, to see three young men come in among them so unexpectedly.'

For the next fortnight he prayed at every opportunity, underground at his work and on the surface. One evening he and a friend agreed to go to the top of an old croft and pray for pardon, and to stay the night there unless they found it. They remained for hours but it came on to rain, they got disheartened and went home. However, the third time he went to the class-meeting, he began to feel peace and love rising in his heart. He felt like the blind man regaining his sight, who at first could 'see men as trees, walking'. Before the meeting closed, he knew that the Lord had pardoned and accepted him. He felt within him the beginning of a new life.

Mr Tyack was appointed to the St Agnes circuit in 1850; he met William Murrish towards the end of the year. William was then a class leader and Sunday school superintendent, and besides the Sunday services, he attended the prayer meeting on Saturday evenings, the preaching service on Friday evenings and cottage meetings on the other evenings of the week. He worked in the mine and cultivated the two or three meadows around his cottage, attending to his pig and cow. He repaired his own and his children's shoes. He also found time to read and to write letters to friends at home and relatives overseas.

Mr Tyack suggested that they should write to each other for their mutual benefit and they kept up the correspondence until the miner's death. The letters are mostly about spiritual matters, though William sometimes refers to his working life. As a miner, he was a tributer, paid a percentage of the value of the ore he raised. In October 1853 he writes: 'I feel thankful to say the Lord has greatly prospered me in the mine lately - I told you we had done pretty well; but I did not know then that we had got so much, by a good deal, as we really had - more than £95 per man, the two months.' A few months before he had hardly known how he could feed his family.

In 1856 there was a revival in the villages round about. At Penhallow, William writes, 'eighteen or twenty, I believe, have been brought in,' at Rose 'between thirty or forty members have been added.' No one thought there would be any revival at Bolingey, but after the Sunday meeting 'one young woman went away weeping aloud. Monday night we had three penitents ... Tuesday, more affected. Wednesday, a blessed time: three conversions and several more impressed. One married man fell like a stone, and wrestled in agony till he was made happy ... Pray, O, pray for us, that the work may go on!' His class increased from eleven to between thirty and forty.

Although in the prime of life, he began to be affected by the miners' disease of dust on the lungs. He had difficulty breathing and his strength gradually diminished. 'I am on the doctor's list ... He has sent a message to me today, not to work till I see him.' He knew the course of the disease. 'I never saw a miner begin to fail in the way that I am, who ever did much work afterwards; though we may have known some who have lived for several years and done some light work.' He hoped to be spared a little, for the sake of his wife and five children, and the fifty members in his two classes. 'I look at it calmly - but, at the same time, seriously.'

In April 1860 he writes: 'For the last eight weeks, I have been laid aside by affliction - inflammation - partially of the lungs. I was confined to the bed for seventeen days, and since I have been able to come down, my recovery has been very slow. I still am an invalid - and when I shall be otherwise, the Lord only knows. But I feel thankful to know that I am in his hands.' He could move only a few yards from the house. 'As soon as I can, I shall endeavour, as the sailors say, to "make the chapel." It is a new thing for me to be kept away eight or nine weeks from the place I have attended so many hundreds of times.'

At Christmas he wrote to Mr Tyack: 'Perhaps you have been ready to say in this cold time we have been passing through - "How is William getting on, I wonder, poor fellow?" - He is still in the land of the living, I am thankful to say; and still able to write a few lines to one who has stuck as close to him, for many years, as a brother.' He wrote to his friends at the chapel a letter to be read out at their Watch Night service, and in his diary on January 1st, 1861, he wrote, 'I can see no other probability than that this year will be my last.'

On the last day of the month he reached his birthday. 'Forty-three years of mercies! Can I not thank God for my birth? Yes, truly!' Mr Tyack visited him, for what proved to be the last time, at Easter. He found him very weak, though still able to dress and be below stairs; he was 'upon the Rock,' peaceful and happy in God. He died on the sixth of May, 1861, about twelve o'clock at noon.

The Wesleyan Chapel

CHAPTER FOURTEEN

Mingoose chapel was built in 1851. It came within the St Agnes circuit and the Reverend W. Davis Tyack must have watched it going up in the three years that he was minister. The work was done by local inhabitants, in their own time after they had finished mining or farming. James Tredinnick claimed to have helped in the building, but as he was only four or five at the time he probably did no more than carry a few stones. They were quarried from the downs and taken in carts up over the hillside and along the track to the site, which was leased from the Enys estate. The lease was made out in the name of James's grandfather, 'James Tredinnick and others', the carrier who lived in Scoll Lane.

They built in the plain and simple style that other Cornish Methodists used all over the county, four solid stone walls beneath a slate roof. At the front was a double door set back in a porch beneath a rounded arch, a plaque above and a window on each side. The window-light above the door was the only elaborate feature of the building, a concave semi-circle of glass held together within tracery. The plaque was a yard across, with the word WESLEYAN curved around the top, the word CHAPEL through the middle and the date 1851 around the bottom. The letters had the solidity of the period; in the date 1 looked like 7. On either side were two tall arched windows, three panes wide and six panes high, with the glass in the arch above divided again by overlapping tracery.

When it was still a chapel, the point of the roof seemed rather off-centre, as though the building was leaning a little, slipping downhill into the valley. This peak was always yellowy-orange with lichen; the slates were grey and blotchy where they had been cemented over, the walls dark brown in the rain, pink in the sunlight. The doors were green, as was the gate in the front wall. There were a few trees around and an evergreen in the front, most of it dead on the side exposed to the south-west wind. It was a building of a sort that you see all over Cornwall, demonstrating the faith of its builders and the sacrifices they made.

Billy Bray, the miner preacher from St Day, described

building such a chapel. "Sometimes I was forenoon core, and when I had taken my dinner I should go to the chapel and work as long as I could see, and the next day do the same. The next week I should be afternoon core; then I should go up to the chapel in the morning and work until the middle of the day, and then go home and away to the mine. The following week I should be night core; I should then work about the chapel by day and go to the mine by night; and had not the dear Lord greatly strengthened me for the work, I could not have done it."

Not everyone in Mingoose was a Methodist. In our house at the time lived the Reverend Edward Montague Hamilton, MA. He had been the curate of St Agnes since 1839; St Agnes had no vicar, as it was only a chapelry in the parish of Perranzabuloe. In 1846 the parishes were divided and Edward Hamilton came to Mingoose as the first vicar of Mount Hawke. From the back door of the house he would have seen straight across the valley to the quarry in the downs and the chapel dominating the top of the hillside. He must have watched all the activity of his neighbours as the building went up. I wonder what his thoughts were. Did he respect and even envy the practical expression that their faith took? After all, his own services at this time were being held in a chapel-of-ease, no more than a little wooden hut at the edge of Mount Hawke. Did he ever meet the Reverend W. Davis Tyack? He must have known of his existence, even if he did not know him socially. Did they ever converse, the Master of Arts and the author of Spiritual Strength and How to Secure It, a word to young converts and to older Christians? ("It should be read by all who are just starting for heaven." - The Primitive Methodist.) I doubt whether they had much contact with each other. Hamilton probably despised the fervour of the Wesleyans and feared their success. Edward Montague Hamilton and W. Davis Tyack: their names represent them well, the one Church of England and a graduate of either Oxford or Cambridge, the other a Cornish Methodist and friend to the miners.

Mr Tyack must have taken some of the earliest services in the chapel. As it was new, he was probably struck by its brightness and cleanliness. Some of the chapels he had preached in were 'fusty, frowsy places, where the windows seem not made to open; the walls were discoloured by damp and mildew; where the dust seems stirred up only to settle down again, without ever being expelled the building; places where old leaves of Bibles and schoolbooks lie about the pulpit-pew; and where the Preacher's eye must ever rest upon heaps of dusty rubbish.'

But Mingoose chapel was light and airy. It had large, south-facing windows and the pews were of varnished pitch pine, with simple, curving bench-ends shaped by the local carpenter. (We have one of them in our kitchen now.) He must have been gratified by its fresh, gleaming look. I hope that he found the appearance of the chapel members equally pleasing. He liked a congregation to be 'well-dressed, but not over-dressed; to present an aspect of sobriety and respectability in deference to the Sabbath-day.' If it was a week-night service, he was satisfied if they came, 'not in their common clothes, but in a sort of second-best, their boots and shoes blacked and shining.' He always noticed the shoes.

The Reverend Edward Montague Hamilton has left no record of his opinions, though when I saw his signature recently, the small tight writing in the St Agnes register of marriages, he suddenly stepped closer across the years.

The chapel congregation at Mingoose had previously worshipped at Goonown, which was then the only chapel in St Agnes. The new society was formed by taking fifty-nine members from the Goonown society. The membership grew to its highest point in 1859, when there were ninety-one members (more than double the total population of the present day). There were also about eighty children attending class in the chapel building. The following year the Sunday school was added, a smaller replica of the chapel, huddled against the far side like a small mushroom against a large one.

There were services each Sunday morning and evening, and Sunday school for the children in the afternoon. The minister either came from St Agnes (Mr Tyack left after the customary three years and went to Devonport) or was one of the local preachers. These men were often, like Billy Bray, miners during the week and preachers on Sundays. They were known for their eloquence, delivering a sermon without notes in the same language and the same tone of voice that they would use in everyday life. Ernest Landry recalled one of them, 'an old chap called Dunstan'. He enlivened his sermons with homely touches and asides. Jonah was wearing miners' hob-nailed boots, which was why the whale cast him up. When Daniel was thrown into the lions' den, the preacher turned the den into a pit and said he expected a lot of Cornish chaps were down there, too, searching for tin. His humour was appreciated by the young people, but the older generation thought he had too much imagination.

A local preacher who came for the morning service would be taken home for dinner by one of the congregation. In Mingoose he went back to the Tredinnicks at Mingoose House. One Sunday at Porthtowan's chapel on the hill the stewards asked Mrs Wicks if she would give dinner to the preacher. She cooked a duck and three pounds of spare rib. The preacher passed up his plate three times; there wasn't much left when he had finished. He then asked Mr Wicks if he could lie down and meditate on the sermon he was to preach at Mawla in the evening. He was left in the best room on the couch and was soon fast asleep. They woke him up for tea and thought that he wouldn't want much to eat after his dinner, but he ate another hearty meal. When he was leaving, Mr Wicks couldn't help passing a comment. "You ought to preach a good sermon in to Mawla," he said, "after all that meditation."

Joe Wicks himself was one of the Sunday school teachers. He was a small, wiry, old man; although he was not an underground miner, he had the reputation of understanding tin. ('He knew tin' was high praise.) He used to collect the ore from the cliffs, letting himself down the cliff-face on a rope tied to a miner's drill driven

The chapel interior

Some of the chapel congregation in about 1948

into the rocks at the top. He had a bag or 'frail' around his neck and filled it with pieces of tin-bearing rock which he knocked off with a hammer and gad. A small frail full of ore represented a good day's work. When he had accumulated a hundredweight, he would load it on his donkey and take it down to the tin-streaming works on the Portreath road.

The boys of the class used to take specimens of rock to Sunday school. He would weigh them in his hands and talk about what they were; he could tell just where they came from. The whole lesson would pass talking about tin and other minerals, and he was very knowledgeable, too, about animals and birds, wild flowers and plants. Ernie Landry and the rest of the boys' class were very good at keeping him talking, until there was hardly time for a bible reading at the end of the lesson.

At Mingoose chapel the anniversary of the Sunday school was always celebrated on the second Sunday in May, the Sunday school tea-treat took place on the second Saturday in July and the Harvest Festival was on the second Sunday in October. These dates never varied, and they were the same as those at two other chapels in the district, Silverwell and Mawla. Before the First World War a Hungarian band always provided the music. They came to Truro for the summer and hired themselves out for tea-treats and other celebrations. They never came back after the war and the chapel hired local bands, from St Agnes and often from Indian Queens. The children had tea in the field below the chapel or in the paddock

Harvest festival at the chapel

Lizzie Shirdy, who frequented all the tea-treats in the early years of the twentieth century

of Mingoose House. They were given Cornish splits and saffron buns as big as dinner plates. There were races and games in the fields and they went in procession up to the Victory Inn, through Towan Cross and back, carrying the Sunday school banner. The day ended with the Serpentine Walk, the moment that the young people had been waiting for. It was the chance of the year for boy and girl to declare an interest in each other. The couples held hands and followed the band as it snaked around the field. All eyes were watching to see who paired off with whom. The bandsmen were then treated to a glass of beer at The Miners' Arms when it was still an inn.

One old lady who frequented all the tea-treats was known as Lizzy Shirty or Shirdy. She wore an enormous shawl that completely covered her, and she had a big wart on the side of her face. She used to sell small things to the children, including photographs of herself. The children liked to see Lizzy Shirty, Ernest Landry said, and people gave her buns and treated her well.

The tea-treat of 1913 took place below the chapel and a photograph was taken of the people of Mingoose seated on pews at trestle tables, with the fields of the valley beyond them and the Victory Inn on the skyline. James Tredinnick, patriarchal with his white beard and tall black hat, is right in the centre. He turns to face the camera although by now he is almost blind. It is the year of Winnie's death and some of her daughters are on the left. Behind James and serving tea are two young ladies in white, Fanny May and her friend Ada Polglaze, both wearing splendid hats. The Hungarian bandsmen in their military uniforms stand at the edge of the group.

The fashionable hats were so wide-brimmed that when the Tredinnick girls sat together in their pew in chapel they had to sit and stand in sequence or they would have knocked them off. When they were young, revival meetings were held at the chapel with special services every night for six weeks. Edwin remembered scores of people being converted. When they decided to commit themselves to Jesus they went forward to the communion rail; some would become very excited. There were two sisters, one of whom went up to seek forgiveness and the other went to clasp her round the waist in praise of God. She was so overjoyed that she threw her arms up and knocked the oil lamp. It flew out amongst the

people, all aflame. Someone grabbed it and carried it outside, where the flames were quickly extinguished.

The great days of the chapel were in the eighteen-sixties. From then onwards the numbers gradually declined. In 1873 there were forty-two members of the society. Many emigrated in the early years of the last century. Mr Tredinnick slowly counted the number who left the Sunday school in the year before he went to California, pausing to remember each name and visualise each face. He counted up to nine, nine young fellows who had left within six months. "What a drain it was on the adult class!" he said.

Several of them went to Bute, Montana. Although they were chapel boys, they were not all honest. Some of them broke into the Assay House of the mine one night to take a sample that they could present as their own, so that their lower-grade ore would be over-valued. As a result of this, they split up and went separate ways.

Mr Retallack's father, Jack, was one of the group. "There was Joe Yelland ... Feather Brochure."

"Feather Brochure?"

Roland repeated it again, distinctly. "Father Bro'shire, or Brokenshire ... Marshall Solway - Pep knew him, she nursed him at the end." He hadn't stayed in America, but came back after a few years like many of the others. Pep had gone to him when he was dying, in the cottage where he had been born. She made him nice and tidy in his bed. He was wearing a shirt; he had never worn

Eddie Tredinnick leading the procesion through Mingoose in 1935

ABOVE
Looking towards the other side of
the valley from above the chapel
RIGHT
Mingoose Chapel after its
conversion to a dwelling

pyjamas in his life. He had a tiny bald head, like a shrivelled apple. "Do you want your cap back on?" she asked him. "I believe I do," he said. He lay there with the bedclothes pulled up to his nose and two big blue eyes peering over the top, a floppy cap on his head. Outside the hens were clucking and a rooster crowed, just as they had no doubt when he came into the world.

Eventually there weren't enough people for the services to continue and they kept only the Anniversary and the Harvest Festival. When we came here, the Sunday school was still open and Susan, Frances and Stephen attended for a while. They sang hymns and listened to The Wind in the Willows, read to them by the great-great-grandson of William Murrish. Sue had a prize for attendance: The Tale of Little Pig Robinson by Beatrix Potter (the only Beatrix Potter book with a Cornish connection, inspired by a visit to Falmouth). There is a label in the front, very bright in gold, red and blue with a design of pillars and arches. It says MINGOOSE SUNDAY SCHOOL, PRESENTED to SUSAN BRANFIELD, 13th MAY 1962. It must have been one of the last Sunday School Anniversaries.

The children grew older and the Sunday school closed. There were no more children to take their place. The chapel was now a shell, lovingly cared for by Carrie Yelland. It was less cared for by Martin, who fired a shot from a .22 rifle through one of the windows. He also frightened the children with his gun. They came tearing back from the downs where they had been playing to say that Mr Yelland had been shooting at them. Pep went and spoke to him.

Martin never worked regularly. He would go across to the Scillies from time to time, to mend clocks and watches. He sometimes phoned us with a message for his mother, to say when he was coming home. He was handy at mending anything. During the war he was working on Eddie Tredinnick's car, lying underneath it, when a ministry official sought him out. He had heard that he was a good instrument maker and offered him a job making equipment for the cockpit panels of aircraft. The wages were high. "I'd have to leave Cornwall?" asked Martin from under the car. "Yes." "And work in a factory?" "Yes." "I couldn't go out and do as I like, when I like?" "Well, no." "Then I shan't take it," said Martin, and he wouldn't come out from beneath the car until the man had gone.

Doing what he liked when he liked was what mattered to him. He liked to wander about underground in the old mines and at South Crofty, which was then working. He would join a shift going down in the cage; everyone knew him and he knew his way around. When they tightened their security arrangements after an accident and wouldn't let him go down any more, he was very indignant and claimed it infringed his rights as a tinner.

He used to drive around in an old car, and at one time for several months he kept a mattress tied to the roof and flopping over the windscreen. He had a length of rubber hose which went from Rose Cottage across the road, high up amongst the trees, to a

In 1948 Jack Berryman, leader of Mingoose Sunday School since Eddie Tredinnick's departure for the United States, decided to replace the tea-treat with an outing to Carbis Bay.

pump driven by a petrol engine in the opposite field. It kept going night and day. It had no obvious purpose, other than to annoy the neighbours.

He died suddenly when he was only fifty. He had driven with a friend out on to Cuba Downs, where he still had a shed from the Wheal Mangle days. He got out of the car to go to the shed and then came back for the keys which he had forgotten. He said that he felt unwell and that he was going to die. His friend ran down to Mingoose Cottage to phone the doctor. She went back and found him sitting in the car, dead.

His father, Joe Yelland, had died in a similar way, out of doors and at the edge of Mingoose. He had been to a Monday evening class-meeting at St Agnes and was walking home when he collapsed and died near Spain Cottage.

There were now only three members of the chapel society left: Edwin Tredinnick and his sisters, May Morrison at Mingoose Cottage and Carrie Yelland at Rose Cottage. They were all over seventy and the maintenance of the hundred-year-old building was too much for them. The Methodist church entered into negotiations with the Enys estate and surrendered the lease three years before it was due to expire. The chapel was put up for sale.

Animals of the Valley, Cliffs and Shore

CHAPTER FIFTEEN

The miners who emigrated to the States could sometimes afford to come home for a three months' holiday. On their return they would often buy themselves a dog and a gun. When Edwin Tredinnick's elder brother Herbert came back from California, he liked to go shooting. The two lads would get up at half-past three in the morning and walk down the valley, where the mines were still working. They would climb to the top of Mulgram Hill and go along the cliffs to Porthtowan. There were plenty of rabbits in the valley and on the downs.

Sometimes the miners back from the States would get permission from a farmer to go rabbiting on his land, sometimes they went poaching; they usually delayed buying a gun licence. A miner called Joel Gill came home with a friend who was a ganger on the railways in America, and they spent nearly all their time shooting. Joel's father worked as a quarryman on the Tehidy estate, and his mother was afraid that if he was caught his father would lose his job. She bought a licence for him and made him put it in his tobacco box in his pocket.

One day the two men were ferreting on a place belonging to Cap'n Prisk from Manor Farm. Cap'n Prisk's son saw them and told Constable Menhier that this was his chance to catch them, as neither would have a licence. When they saw Constable Menhier coming, Joel picked up his gun and ran. The constable chased after him. He ran across the manor field, down the adit and up the other hillside. Just before he got to the top he sat down on a bank and waited. When the constable reached him, Gill said, "You've got a lot more breath than I have, Menhier."

"I'd have caught you even if I'd had to chase you up to Scorrier," replied the constable. "Now I'll trouble 'ee for that licence I know you haven't got."

"Wait a bit, Menhier," said Joel, and he started to search his pockets, taking out his pouch, his keys, his money.

"I don't want any damn nonsense from you, Gill," said Menhier. "I know very well you haven't got a licence."

Gill continued searching through his pockets, eventually

taking out his tobacco box. He opened it up, unfolded the piece of paper and passed it to Menhier. When the constable had got over his surprise, he said, "You damn fool, Gill. What did you run for?"

"Free country," said Gill. "What did you run for?"

Ernest Landry, who told the story of Constable Menhier (he made the name sound like an Old Testament prophet, rhyming it with Isaiah), said that the rabbits on the cliffs would lie up in 'seats' instead of going into burrows. They would get under the heather and bite off the tops, to make it more like a nest. After a few days the heather would die ('quail', he called it), drawing attention to the hiding place. If you approached from downwind, you could pounce on these patches of dead heather and catch the rabbits underneath with your hands. He sometimes caught ten or twelve in a morning.

When he was young, a country boy could make quite a bit of pocket money. There was a ready market for fresh-caught rabbits at sixpence or eight pence each. He trapped them with snares set in the runs or with a length of net in a gateway, to catch them as they came out of the fields by night. A cousin of his worked full-time as a trapper. He would pay up to a hundred pounds for the trapping rights on a farm. He worked night and day, sometimes never taking his clothes off for a whole week, but he saved enough money from snaring rabbits to buy a farm at St Erth.

The fields are still overrun with rabbits, despite the myxomatosis which nearly wiped them out at one time. Our cats sometimes brought them home, staggering up the drive with heads held high, the bodies as big as themselves hanging from their mouths. "No, Roland," said Pep. "I'm not going to make a stew."

Badgers and foxes thrive in the valley. We see them at night in the headlights of the car as we're coming home. One evening, walking back from the beach in the half-light, I heard grunting noises approaching and met two badgers head-on. I stood aside and they trundled past, grumbling loudly. At the side of footpaths there are often 'snuffle-holes' where an animal has scrapped away the earth, after grubs or earth worms. Some are toilet-holes with grey droppings, full of fur and the shards of beetles. Suddenly in the 'tunnel' I come across the sharp stink of a fox, the smell held between the overhanging trees. At night we hear the mating call of a vixen echoing eerily across the valley.

A postcard view of the valley in about 1903

One afternoon in early summer, I saw from the garden a fox coming down the opposite hillside. It followed a track to the old quarry, where the stone was taken for the chapel. It reappeared every afternoon at about the same time. I told the naturalist Roger Burrows, who came to watch from our side of the valley. He said it was a vixen whose cubs had probably been born in an earth some distance away. She had now hidden them in the quarry. It provided good cover as it had been used as a tip in the past and contained sheets of corrugated iron covered with rubble and grown over with brambles and hawthorns. The mother would lie up in another hide during the day and come to join her cubs in the evening. She would hunt at night; she would still be feeding them and would be very hungry. She probably ate mostly worms and beetles, voles and mice, perhaps a few rabbits. Mrs Rashleigh's hens, coming up to the top of the field, were no more than a few feet away, but they were quite safe. She wouldn't kill right on the doorstep of her cubs' hiding-place. The hens scratched around, quite oblivious - as was Mrs Rashleigh - to the presence of the dreaded foxes.

We saw another adult vixen visiting the quarry, possibly the unmated sister of the mother, and we watched the cubs come out to play. They nosed around amongst the stone and heather, giving little rushes forward and back but never going far away. Sometimes the mother came out with them. She would lie curled up in the slanting sunlight, snapping at them if they bothered her. Once we went up on the downs and approached the quarry. A cub came along the path and we stood still. It stopped and looked at us, full

A donkey grazes in the lower part of the valley, with East Wheal Charlotte in the background

of curiosity. Its face was very alert, its fur quite red and its eyes bright blue. There was a sense of encounter, a thrill of wonder at a different way of life existing alongside our own. Then the fox cub turned and ambled back along the path.

In the early autumn someone shot the mother and at least one of the cubs. One or two of the family might have survived. Farmers have always destroyed foxes, although in the opinion of most naturalists the foxes do not deserve their reputation as vicious killers. Ernest Landry shot many of them on his farm. They used to breed in the mine adits, and when they were weaning the cubs they would bring them up from the cliffs and put them in the rabbit sets in the hedges round the farm. As a boy, he used to dig them out and sell them to the hunt at Scorrier House. The last lot that he dug out he sold to some show people at Redruth's Whitsun Fair and they put them on display in a cage.

He also observed them and came to sympathise with them. He remembered watching two foxes, a dog and a bitch, working a furze brake together, searching for a rabbit. The vixen drove the rabbit out and the fox took it up; they shared the kill between them without any quarrelling. One evening he saw four or five cubs searching the top of the cliffs. He wondered what they were picking up and found that they were eating what he called 'big dew snails'.

But the foxes not only ate rabbits and snails; they also ate his chickens. One year he had lost several. He knew where the fox cubs were and he made a hide nearby. He took his gun and crept into the hide just before daybreak. Before long he heard a sound and the vixen came over the bank with a chicken. She gave a peculiar calling noise and the five young ones came out. Soon the feathers were flying, while the mother looked over each cub, smelling and licking it. He could have shot them all, but he didn't have the heart. He stayed and watched them.

A seal cave, with the remains of the Eltham

Another time he was out with his gun and he saw a fox moving very slowly. He wondered why it didn't disappear quickly, as he knew it had seen him. He followed and caught up with it. Its leg was trapped in a rabbit gin; it had pulled the peg out of the ground and took the gin with it. He pressed its head down with the butt of his gun and put his foot on the gin to open it. The fox was released and ran off. "That was another time I let a fox go," he said. "I thought he had had pain enough."

One evening he went down a path, the only one on the cliffs, and on the rocks at the bottom a fox was searching for gulls' eggs or young birds. To get up the cliff it would have had to pass him. It chose instead to jump into the sea. He could have shot it in the water but he watched it swim around the point to the next beach, a distance of about a quarter of a mile. It came out of the water, shook itself like a dog and trotted off into the caves.

The foxes in the valley were not hunted by the foxhounds, as it was too near the coast; the fox might have led the dogs over the edge of the cliff. But on occasions the Four Burrow Hunt followed a fox into Mingoose and lost it. The hounds milled about on the hillside; the whipper-in called to get them together but they seemed out of control. Riders cantered to and fro across the downs. A huntsman in black jacket and white breeches came crashing down the lane at the side of the house, shielding his face from the low, overhanging branches. Peter was about ten years old. He stood on the bank and shouted boldly, "Abolish blood sports!" The man was taken by surprise at this sudden apparition. "The fox enjoys it," he shouted back, and pushed his horse on to catch up the others. For hours after the riders had gone there were dogs wandering lost about the valley.

Sometimes along the coast or in the cove at Chapel Porth grey seals can be seen 'bottling', sitting up in the water in order to look around. They are very curious and take as much interest in swimmers as the swimmers take in them. In Ernie Landry's day, they were numerous. There was a cave in the cliffs which bounded his farm, where they used to breed. He visited this cave every year for over fifty years, up until the end of the nineteen-forties. Sometimes there were only five or six seals born there, in other years as many as twenty.

The cave was rocky at the entrance and opened out into a wide sandy beach inside. At high tide the sea reached the end of the cave, but as it was some way into the cliff the waves were not strong enough to batter the baby seals against the rock. He would stand at the end of the tunnel, looking seawards to watch the mother seals swimming into the cave on the incoming tide to nurse their young. He used to take visitors to the farm down a mine shaft which was fitted with ladders, and through the old workings of the mine. The tunnels led to the cave, which had been used as an adit. If the sea was rough, the huge breakers filled the entrance and rushed up on to the sandy beach. One Christmas day he went down the shaft and through the workings to the tunnel. There on the sand inside the cave were over seventy fully-grown seals. He guessed by the smell of their breath that they had had a good feed of fish out to sea, and had come in to sleep it off.

Whistlers and Whinners

CHAPTER SIXTEEN

St Agnes men are known as 'cuckoos'. The story is a local variation on the story of the wise men of Gotham, who tried to capture a cuckoo - and thus prolong the summer - by building a wall around it. In Ernest Landry's version it was given a precise location. The men were building turf hedges at Teagle's farm. It was the month of April and a cuckoo flew by, skimming over the top of the bank. A man called Tonkin said, "If we was one turf higher, we should have had 'un." That was how the men of St Agnes gained their nickname.

Mr Landry reckoned that all birds were more numerous when he was a boy. The winters were much colder then and enormous flocks of whinners (redwing) and fieldfare came from the north. There were great flocks, too, of peewits and whistlers (lapwings and golden plovers). If the cold weather continued for long the lapwings would get very thin, until they had no flesh on them at all and he had seen them die by the hundred. Some people in winter used to go bush-beating, catching the birds when they were roosting. He'd known them catch fifty or sixty birds in a night, gravers (blackbirds) and thrushes. They used to pluck them and roast them in the oven and very nice eating they were too.

Unlike the lapwings, the golden plovers always stayed plump, even in the coldest spell, and were good birds to eat. But the best birds of all were the rooks. Near his farm was a smallholding called the Rookery, with a plantation of fir trees where the rooks used to build. People would shoot the young ones just before they were ready to fly. He sometimes shot out a dozen and took them home, and his mother would stuff them with parsley and breadcrumbs and cook them in a big dish in the Cornish range. They never smelled or tasted at all 'rooky'.

When he was ploughing with the horses, there were always thousands of gulls following behind. They were looking for earthworms, which are good for the soil and it was difficult to drive the birds away. A lot of wagtails and titlarks also followed the plough. "What we call in Cornish teeter-larks," he said, though I felt it was not so much Cornish, rather that his delicacy prevented

The Cornish range in Mingoose Cotttage

him from saying 'tit' in the presence of my wife. Pied wagtails were called 'tinners', perhaps because they are black and white like St Piran's flag with its white seam of tin on a black ground. They were more welcome, as they were looking for wire-worms.

As a boy, he always enjoyed taking a horse to be shod. Daniel Laity had been a mining blacksmith and when the mine closed he opened his own blacksmith's shop. He did a lot of work for the farmers, sharpening harrow tines and plough coulters, and he had a smallholding with an orchard. He kept a single-barrelled shotgun to scare the birds off his fruit trees and he would let the boys use the gun while he was shoeing the horse. Bullfinches were the most destructive and he was always pleased if they shot a few.

"There were hundreds of bullfinches in those days," Ernest said. "Today you rarely see one. I wonder what happened to them."

"You shot them all," said Pep.

He thought about it for a bit. "There were so many, you never believed they could all disappear."

He used to collect peewits' eggs when he was a boy. There was a good market for them and it was all extra pocket money. He would also trap snipe down in the marsh and sell them at sixpence each to the two ladies who kept a game shop in Redruth. Once he earned sixpence from the vicar of Mount Hawke and had a morning off school into the bargain.

122

The successor to the vicars who lived in our house, now established in the rectory next door to the church, was the Reverend John Ching Barfett, known as 'the sporting parson'. He was a hunting and shooting man, a follower of the Four Burrow hounds. One morning, out with his gun, he met young Ernie Landry on his way to school. "Any birds about, boy?" he asked. "Yes," said Ernie. "When I came up to the top of the hill at Short Cross there was a flock of whistlers in Mrs Hitchen's field." "Come along and show me." "I'll be late for school." "Never mind that," said the parson. "I'll make it right."

It was a cold, frosty morning. The golden plover were still in the field and the parson crept towards them behind the furze bushes. Ernie wondered why he took so long, but he told him afterwards that he was waiting to get two in a line. He fired and two were on the ground; he shot another as they flew up. The parson was delighted, he had three golden plover. "Come on, boy," he said. "We'll go up Parc Shady way now, I might get a shot at a woodpigeon or two."

The Reverend John Ching Barfett, vicar of Mount Hawke 1900-1914, the 'sporting parson'

He had two or three shots at woodpigeons, but without success. They went on to Gover Valley to look for snipe. There were plenty there. He fired all the cartridges he had and bagged just one bird. "A costly business, this snipe," said young Ernie.

When he got to school it was between playtime and dinner time. Ernie slipped into his desk and the parson went to the front of the class and spoke to Mr Richards, the headmaster. Later, the master came over to him. "You had a good time this morning, boy," he said. "Parson gives you a good name for knowing birds."

There were oyster-catchers on the beach. They were called 'sea pies' because of their black and white plumage like a magpie's, and they fed on small crab-like insects known as 'sea lice'. Sometimes flocks of woodcock would arrive on the beach, so exhausted after a long sea passage that they could not rise over the cliffs. There were two pairs of peregrine falcons that nested there year after year. Each season they raised a brood, but the young birds never stayed in the area. They fed almost entirely on pigeons. Ernie climbed to their nests a few times, but he never saw the young fed with anything bearing fur. The parents tore the pigeons into small pieces for the young to swallow. There were buzzards, kestrels and ravens also nesting on the cliffs. The buzzards lived off the rabbits and the ravens ate carrion. They both tore the food apart for their young, but the cormorants on the rocks fed their young with whole fish, sometimes too large for them to swallow. A cormorant was known as a 'Jack Cocking'.

The Cornish chough could still be seen in the area, but it was already rare. There were never more than three, and he never saw them anywhere but on the cliff face. They never nested nor raised any young, and disappeared altogether after a few years. In The Cornish Chough T.O. Darke describes how they had been facing extinction throughout the nineteenth century, gradually disappearing from the whole length of the south Cornish coast. By Ernest Landry's time they were just holding on along the north coast, between Hell's Mouth and Tintagel. In the nineteen-forties they declined rapidly. In 1941 fifteen choughs were seen together near Newquay, but in 1946 only two broods were recorded. There were three in 1947 and these were to be the last. The survivors from these broods lived on through the fifties and sixties, never breeding successfully. By 1957 one pair only remained, for ten years haunting the cliffs that had been the home of their ancestors for thousands of years. In 1968 one chough was found dead. The other lingered on into the early seventies, the last of its race.

It was a lovely bird, said Mr Landry. It had glossy black plumage and scarlet beak and legs; its beak was slightly curved. It had more elegance that the other crows. In the air it was a skilful flier, on the ground it would hop, walk and run. It lived on insects and grubs, stabbing its bill into the ground to find its food. Its call was like a jackdaw's, only softer. It liked wild stormy spaces; it needed to be free and unconfined. It had long been adopted as the symbol of Cornwall.

Why was it unable to survive in the twentieth century? He remembered a conversation about the Cornish chough, or 'chaw' as they called it, between his Sunday school teacher, the knowledgeable Mr Wicks, and an old farmer. They said that they had never been plentiful, about a dozen at most in the area. The farmer thought that the peregrine falcons, which he called 'kites' or 'keets', were killing the young ones. Mr Wicks thought that the jackdaws were pushing them out and eating the eggs from their nests.

Their chief enemy would seem to have been man rather than

other birds. From earliest times they were caught and put into cages. They were not only handsome, they would also become very attached to humans. They were shot and sold as game. When the gin traps were set for the rabbits on the cliffs they were often caught by mistake, more so than any other coastal birds, for they probed in the soil for insects just where the traps were hidden. They were shot for sport or for their skins, to be stuffed and put into glass cabinets. Their eggs were taken by collectors and the rarer they became, the more worthwhile it was for an impoverished miner to climb down the cliffs and rob the nests. A clutch was worth a pound or two at the end of the nineteenth century.

But this direct persecution they could probably have survived, for many other species were similarly treated. What was harder to survive were the indirect effects of human beings upon their way of life. They thrived best when agriculture was not very efficient, when large areas of land on the cliff tops were used as rough grazing for sheep and cattle. Their numbers began to decrease as fields were ploughed for corn right to the cliff edge. They lived entirely on insects and particularly on ants. There were fewer ant hills in ploughed fields than undisturbed downland.

It made little difference to the jackdaws, their rivals for space. They eat corn as well as insects and they prospered at the expense of the choughs. They were more adaptable, too, in their choice of nesting sites. They would build in chapels and engine houses, whereas the choughs remained on the cliffs. Jackdaws nest today under the eaves of our house, having edged out the starlings that in

turn had edged out the house sparrows that were the only occupants when we first arrived.

Like the chough, the peregrine falcon too was over-specialised, feeding almost entirely on pigeons. During the war the Air Ministry believed they were a threat to the carrier pigeons used by the RAF, and all known breeding sites were destroyed and the birds shot. (It was true that they liked racing pigeons; Ernest Landry saw them catch many.) Yet surprisingly, within a few years after the end of the war they had re-established themselves. The peregrine falcons were prepared to travel and re-colonise, unlike the Cornish choughs, which never moved far from where they were born and so the stock was never revitalised.

Suddenly in the mid-fifties the falcon population began to decline again, until by the sixties none was breeding in Cornwall. There was no shortage of the feral pigeons on which they lived. But the pigeons ate corn, and the corn contained insecticides from the chemical dressings increasingly used in agriculture. The insecticides were toxic to birds.

In the seventies the peregrine falcons slowly re-established themselves for a second time, and they can be seen again perched high on the cliffs along the coast or swooping out over the sea. Choughs, too, have reappeared on the Lizard in the twenty-first century, breeding successfully.

There are more buzzards than ever, but not as many as owls. The call of owls was a regular sound at night, a background noise that was taken for granted. There always used to be several young

owls in the garden on summer evenings; they made a noise like the excited yapping of puppies. One year a tawny owl laid her eggs in an old pigeon's nest in the garden. When they had hatched she would stay away all day and come swooping into the tree at dusk. The two chicks were forever falling out of the nest and we had to keep putting them back. They did not seem well-adapted for survival.

There has always been a pair of crows in the valley. I used to think they were ravens, and I'm still not completely sure. They are large and very immobile; they rarely move from the downs, the hawthorn bush by the quarry or the trees by the stream. Something about them, their economy of movement and the way they are always together, make them seem very ancient. And sometimes, instead of a 'caw', there comes from the opposite hillside a most mournful sound. It is like three long sighs, as though they are expressing all the melancholy of a long life. I've seen one of them give this cry. It tucked its head against its breast and seemed to draw the sigh up from the depths of its body, uncurling its head and thrusting it out as the moan came through its beak in three despairing exhalations. Oh, oh ... oh, it sighed.

A bird that has disappeared from Cornwall is the corncrake. It too has been a victim of changes in the use of the land. It liked marshes and rough grazing, the sort of countryside that has diminished. The noise it made used to be one of the sounds of summer, according to Ernest Landry. Around hay-making time it was constant throughout the day and late into the evening, as frequent as the call of the cuckoo, though in recent years the cuckoo has been heard less often.

I went into the garden one very still evening in early June, when the sun had set but the sky was still light. The sea was a very pale silver-blue, with darker bands across the bottom of the V at the end of the valley. There was a strong scent of honeysuckle at the back of the house. Every sound carried far: there was the clacking of the miniature water-wheel in the stream at Mingoose Vale, the crash of a wave on the beach. And then I heard this strange haunting call.

It was a double croak, two deep, guttural notes sounding very clear in the still air. It was a very arresting sound. It wasn't a jackdaw or a crow, it was much more unusual. I stopped to listen. The call was repeated more loudly, as though the bird was flying in from the sea. I tried to see it, but all the trees were in leaf and darkness had spread through the bottom of the valley. It kept calling. It seemed to be low, close to the ground and following the stream through the fields beyond the trees. It was moving slowly, too slowly, I thought, to be flying, and I wondered whether it was landing and then flying on. The disembodied voice passed through the valley and the bird seemed to settle in the fields of Mingoose Farm. It was getting too dark to go and look for it, but it continued calling into the night.

Each evening it could be heard again. I traced it to a field opposite the chapel, in the corner between Scoll Lane and the road to St Agnes. The grass was uncut, but it was not good hay; it had been grazed earlier and was rather patchy. The bird kept calling and I could pin-point where it was without seeing it. It kept very low and never moved, although I waited quite a while. I had no idea what it was, but there was something very different and very compelling about its call. I asked Roger Burrows, who came and listened and said that it was a corncrake.

Then the RSPB came with listening dishes and set up a miniature Goonhilly to record the presence of the bird. Its sighting was officially listed. It stayed all through the summer, a single bird without a mate. It had strayed perhaps - like Paddy Murphy - from Ireland where it is still fairly common in the west. In August it flew away.

128

Flowers and Insects

CHAPTER SEVENTEEN

On a spring morning the sun shines into the valley, creating strong patterns of light and shade as the overlapping hillsides recede to the sea. The moors are still the tawny colour of winter. In the bottom of the valley the pine trees make a patch of dark green. Elsewhere there is the light green of new growth on hawthorn and willow, the cream and pink of the opening buds of sycamores, a white drift of blackthorn blossom. And rising up the hills and pushing into the heathland are great splashes of deep yellow, the blaze of gorse in bloom, set off against the blue of the sea and sky.

The gorse or furze is the plant I associate most with the valley. It blossoms first in January, a scattering of flowers on the dead-looking bushes along the tops of hedges, encroaching into fields and on the downs. It blossoms again in April and this time it colours the hillsides with its deep egg-yolk yellow. When the sun warms the flowers, they smell of coconut. It blossoms a third time, later in the summer.

My mother always stayed with us at Easter and she 'knew flowers'. She looked for heath spotted orchids alongside the path and on the north-facing slope of the valley. They push up above the heather, pink pyramids of flowers. Usually on the same day towards the end of April she would find the first lousewort, another pink flower growing close to the ground at the edge of the path or amongst mine waste. Milkwort with tiny pink or blue flowers on short spikes grows in similar places.

She always hoped to see vernal squill. The best place to find it is at Chapel Porth, where the coastal path leaves the beach and climbs up towards Wheal Coates. This side of the cove faces south-west and gets a lot of sun, and the spring squill flowers early, where the well and the chapel used to be. Star-shaped and pale bluebell-coloured, they lie close to the grass and spread a blue haze over the cliffs.

On the other side of the valley the wind has blown sand on to the slopes facing north-east, and it is covered with tough wiry grass instead of gorse and heather. A little way inland there are cowslips in the spring and burnet roses later where the grass and

heather meet. Along the side of the path are tormentil, kidney vetch and birds'-foot trefoil, all with yellow flowers, scurvy grass with white flowers and fleshy leaves, and patches of wild thyme. On the banks of the stream are purple loosestrife, fleabane and meadowsweet.

The stream is fresh and unpolluted. The water looks pure enough to drink as it slides over small falls and rushes around bends; there are pools where it hardly seems to move. As I approach, I occasionally see a brown trout darting away like a shadow. Almost invisible bubbles on the surface cast shadows which move in blobs across the bottom. A stalk or bit of debris floats past. Suddenly its speed increases, it dips under the water and up again, and rushes into the flow of the stream, twisting and turning as it disappears into a tunnel of vegetation. There are water-boatmen on the surface and other water insects beneath the stones. Dragonflies hover above in their tilted, helicopter-like flight. The approaches to the American bridge hold back the stream, and in the marsh grow yellow flags among lots of primeval-looking horsetails. There are banks of thrift and water dropwort.

The flower of high summer is the heather. There are three sorts in Chapel Coombe, bright purple bell heather which colours the hillsides in July and the more delicate, pinky-mauve ling. Cross-leaved heath has a cluster of pink bells at the head of the stalk, like a Mabel Lucie Atwell drawing of plump little girls.

Inland, along the roads and footpaths of Mingoose one plant dominates the hedgerow for a short while, to be replaced by the next. The season starts with Alexanders, which Mr Retallack called

'skeets', filling the verges with their tall yellowy-green stems and flowers. It is closely followed by wild garlic or three-cornered leek, which since its introduction in the mid nineteenth century has spread everywhere in Cornwall; we have seen it march like an army down the lane at the side of our house and invade the garden through an undefended stile. Then it is the turn of red campions and bluebells and in June the white lace of cow parsley fills the paths and narrows the roads. Pink purslane, germander speedwell, hedge bedstraw - each has its moment when it flourishes and fades away.

It is the foxglove above all which is the flower of the inland valley. If the gorse captures the spirit of spring, the foxglove evokes early summer and heat. Away from the sea there are tall banks of them against the hedges and in the corner of fields. They line the roadsides, tall spires of purple-pink flowers, open-mouthed and speckled inside. As the tubular bells open from the bottom to the top, the stalks at the roadside lean more and more into the path of the traffic.

Foxgloves are a favourite of the bees and there have always been a few hives in Mingoose. We had them nesting in the bathroom roof, between the corrugated asbestos and the wooden ceiling of the extension. The bees congregated over the bath, where the steam from the hot water would penetrate the boards and warm them. In winter when we were having a bath the heat would wake them and they would start humming. Sometimes, if the bath water was very hot, the honey from the combs would begin to melt and drip through the ceiling, in the cracks between the tongue and groove boards.

Down the hill to Chapel Porth

When they swarmed we realised how numerous they were. At first there were more in the air than usual, buzzing loudly and flying around in a very agitated state. The noise increased until it drowned all other sounds. It gave meaning to the image of the 'beehive' that the old people used to describe the valley in the past. Thousands of bees outside the window darkened the room. They flew to and fro endlessly until a great mass of them left with a queen to found a new colony. The others gradually settled down, but it took several days for them to get back to normal.

Eventually they became diseased. They had diarrhoea and dropped golden shit all over the drive and doorstep. They had previously kept very much to themselves, completely ignoring the human beings with whom they shared the house. But now they became vicious, dive-bombing any person who came in sight. To get into the house we had to run for the door, holding our collars tight to our necks as the kamikaze fighters hurtled down to the attack, buzzing loudly as they came. The children were stung and we had to have the bees destroyed.

We felt there should have been some other way of dealing with the problem. May Morrison, half-seriously, asked if we had kept the bees informed, telling them everything that happened in the house. Had we told them when Peter was born? We didn't think we had. When they were no longer there to control the honey it started to flow down the bathroom walls. We removed the boards of the ceiling and took out bucketfuls of dead bees, basins of wax comb and honey.

They had always lived in the house. Before the extension was built, they lived in the roof. In the space between the slates and the slope of the bedroom ceilings there were yards of old honeycomb, pieces like outsize loofahs stuck side by side. For many years afterwards, each spring, a few scout bees would appear and hover around the guttering, dancing up and down in front of the old entrances. But no new swarm ever followed them to take up residence again, though they use other houses in Mingoose.

The valley is a migration route for butterflies. On a bright and windy day early in September I went for a walk with a friend who is good at recognising them. We saw small whites and speckled woods everywhere, red admirals and small tortoise-shells. There were large whites and common blues, mostly on the coastal heath. We saw a few small coppers, painted ladies and meadow browns, and just one gatekeeper (there would have been hundreds in August) and one peacock, by then mostly hibernating. On the top of the Beacon were about half a dozen each of grayling and wall butterflies, looking very tattered. They were fluttering close to the rocks and were blown about by the wind.

Late one evening in June, I walked down to the beach. The holiday-makers had packed up and left as soon as the sun had disappeared below the horizon. There were no surfers as there were hardly any waves and it was too calm for the anglers. It was still light enough to see and I started to walk along the coastal path. The rocks gave out the heat absorbed during the day. The sea below barely murmured.

The hanging valley above the two caves, and site of the holy well

133

A short way along the path I saw the first phosphorescent glimmer, and then as I turned into the valley which leads down to the two caves, the slopes were covered with tiny points of green light. The glow-worms, beetles rather than worms, were clinging to the heather or to blades of dried grass, holding on with their legs and turning the undersides of their abdomens upwards. The last three segments shone out to the males, the final segment glowing less brightly than the other two.

When she was a girl going home through the lanes in the summer dusk, my mother used to pick a glow-worm out of the hedgerow and put it into her hat, so that anyone approaching would mistake her for a man smoking a cigarette. It might have given her confidence, but it would not have been very convincing and the glow-worm can turn the light out at will.

As I watched, in the combe or dingle where there was once a holy spring, some of the greenish lights on the hillside went out and others came on, as they must have done when there was a chapel over the well and - I like to imagine - a hermit to tend it.

The Ghosts of the Past

CHAPTER EIGHTEEN

I wanted to live by the sea, in a cell where I could write, somewhere wild and remote, where I could walk along the shore and over the cliffs, through moorland and valley. I wanted somewhere exposed to the elements, where the waves roared and the spray flew, where the gales raged in winter. I wanted somewhere that was not too English, somewhere at the edge. Pep wasn't much bothered.

While we were looking for such a place, we rented the chalet at Porthtowan. We intended to search anywhere within a twenty-mile radius, but one of the first houses we saw advertised in the West Briton was only a mile or two from our temporary home. We got the details from Lodge and Thomas, and made arrangements to visit. We drove up the hill out of Porthtowan and along by the workings of Wheal Towan mine and the side of Wheal Charlotte moor to the Victory Inn, where we had stopped once before. We turned down the lane and descended the hill. There was a patchwork of small fields on the opposite slope, with a farm and farm buildings on the skyline. We turned the corner and saw the house for the first time.

It was a raw autumnal evening after a day of rain. The roof and the stone walls were dark with the wet. The trees around it had lost most of their leaves and we saw the house through the bare branches, to which a few brown leaves still clung. The hill rose at the side and some damp brown cattle stood in the field. There was a wrought-iron gate, with elaborate spikes and curls, between two granite posts in a Cornish hedge topped with gorse and fuchsia. I knew without going any further that it was where I wanted to live.

We had stopped right on the bend. I backed and drew off the road in front of the gate. The gate stuck, as it still does, but I managed to open it. We went up the path to the front door and knocked. There was a lot of shuffling and scraping inside until the door suddenly burst free from the jambs against which it had swollen. The two ladies who lived in the house, Miss Crewes and Miss English, explained that everyone usually came to the back door, and we stepped over a pool of water into the hall.

The kitchen was dark and warm from a Rayburn. It was like a farmhouse kitchen, just a stove and a big table, with no water or sink. The beams and ceiling were painted a deep cream, which had turned almost brown with tobacco smoke. There was an enormous mahogany sideboard along one wall. We looked at the other rooms, one each side of the hall at the front and two rooms behind them at the back, the kitchen and the 'dairy' as they called it, linked by a passage which was used as a scullery. The dairy had only a tiny window, about a foot square, covered with perforated zinc instead of glass.

From the hall the stairs went up to a landing, where they branched one way to the bathroom, a very low-ceilinged extension to the rear of the house above the scullery. The other way led to the top landing and a passageway between the bedrooms, three at the front and two at the back. The front bedrooms had panelled doors with door knobs, the back rooms had planked doors with latches. These we were told had been the servants' rooms. If that was so, the Victorian lower middle classes must have lived very close to their servants. We heard about the vicars; they couldn't have turned over in their sleep without the maid knowing.

We went outside the back door into the drizzle. The drive came up from the road to a small yard under the hill. The other side of the yard was formed by a building whose slate roof came right out of the hillside and continued, stepped down, at a lower level. There were double doors to this part, right opposite the back door of the house. This was where the trap had been kept; the pony had been stabled at the far end, under the hill. We followed a path round the coach-house to the garden and stood on the mine-shaft, without knowing what it was. Some stone steps led to a loft, through a low door. The man employed to drive the vicars to church slept here on the hay. He dropped the hay to the pony, next door and below, through a hole in the wall.

I walked on my own to the top of the garden. I couldn't believe that the house was available. It had been on the market for a year at four thousand pounds and no one had bought it. It had been withdrawn for a while and was now offered at three thousand seven hundred. It wouldn't have surprised me if they had asked five thousand. How could you put any price on it at all?

The garden was described in the agents' details as 'mature

but neglected'. There were paths and bushes at different levels on the slope of the hillside, all rather unkempt and wild. I saw the drang running down the side, stone-built and mossy, with branches of trees interlaced above it. I reached the top of the garden and looked back. From this point I was above the level of the roofs. I looked down through ash trees and a wych-elm tree, over the grey slate roofs of the outbuildings and the house and beyond them to the bare slopes of the valley and the misty sea. The brick chimneys were at ground level at one end of the house and high above the trees at the other. The four chimney pots filled the bottom of the V shape of the valley and stood out against the sea.

I was anxious that someone else might make an offer before us. But no one did. We looked at other properties, so that we didn't feel that we had bought the first house that we had seen, but they only confirmed our choice. Sometimes, as we waited to exchange contracts, we wondered; there must be something wrong with it if it had been on the market for a year. We would go for a walk on Wheal Charlotte moor and then feel drawn towards the house. We would come down the lane and look at it once more, to check that it really was as we thought. We tried to come across it unexpectedly, to surprise ourselves into seeing it with fresh eyes. Each time it looked the same: solid and enduring, well-placed on the side of the valley.

The view down the valley

The survey found a lot wrong, but no more than you would expect in an old house and we moved in just after Christmas, on Susan's sixth birthday. It was a day of thick fog; the opposite hillside, the sides of the valley and the sea were blotted out. Everywhere was soaking wet, even though it was not raining. The grass of the front lawn was covered with droplets and the furniture removers left footprints across it, the floors inside the house glistened with moisture, the wallpaper had large patches of damp. The furniture van was parked on the corner and whenever a car came the men had to stop unloading and take the van up the road so that the car could pass. We put the kettle on the Rayburn, but it never boiled and the electric cooker was not yet connected. Nothing worked. Everywhere was wet and cold. Pep wondered what she was doing here.

Once the removal men had gone, the front and back doors could be closed, shutting out the fog. The coal in the stove began to glow red hot and the kettle boiled. The house gradually became warmer and drier. We put our bed in the room from where, when the mist was not curling against the window panes, we could look down the valley to the engine house and the sea. Sue had the little bedroom in the middle at the front of the house, and Frances and Stephen shared a bedroom at the back. The last in a long line of inhabitants had taken possession.

The house had been built early in the nineteenth century, its existence linked to the revival of tin-mining at that time. Wheal Towan, on the road to Porthtowan beyond the Victory Inn, was at the height of its prosperity. It was presumed that the same rich lode of copper continued to the east, and North Towan and East Towan on the moor opposite the Victory Inn and Wheal Tallack behind Tresco Farm were attempts to find it. These mines failed to come up to expectation; some copper ore was found, nearly five hundred tons at East Towan in 1805, but it was not the extension of Wheal Towan that was hoped for. The adventurers were convinced that the seam must continue eastwards and made other efforts to trace it. Wheal Gertrude was one of these attempts.

One day I saw a man in a long black overcoat standing at the gate, looking like Eddie Tredinnick's Spaniard. I went and spoke to him and he introduced himself as Hamilton Jenkin. He came and looked at the shaft in the garden and confirmed that it was

Wheal Gertrude. According to his Mines and Miners of Cornwall, Vol. 11. St Agnes - Perranporth, it was working on a small scale in 1809. Martin Yelland told me that the outbuildings behind the house were referred to by the old men as the 'workshops'. The end nearest the valley was the blacksmith's shop and the other end, before the loft was put in and the stable added, joining the building to the hillside, was the carpenter's shop.

There was a clomb oven by the side of the chimney in the blacksmith's shop. It would not have been normal workshop equipment. It is a round clay oven which would have been filled with furze and lit. When the furze was burnt to ashes and the oven hot, the bread would be put in through the metal door and it would bake as the oven gradually cooled. It suggests that the building was an eighteenth-century cottage, taken over and used as workshops when the mine was opened and the shaft sunk.

The house could have been built at the same time, as the count house of the mine. The count house was where the mine manager or purser lived (sometimes the mine captain, though a mine often had several captains who worked underground). It was where the accounts were kept and the miners paid. It was where the shareholders or adventurers would inspect the books either once a month, once a quarter or twice a year. The count house was usually built in a solid, farmhouse style, with more room and higher ceilings than a cottage. If this was the count house, it would have been built about 1809. I imagine the first woman who lived here, the purser's wife, was called Gertrude and gave her name to the mine.

However, there seem to be one or two objections to this date. It is strange that such a very small and unsuccessful venture as Wheal Gertrude (for they never found the eastward continuation of the copper lodes of Wheal Towan) should have had a count house, when there are no remaining count houses for the other mines. There's not a single building at Wheal Towan, and the scarred and waste ground at its eastern end is now mostly covered with top soil and turned into fields. Perhaps the buildings of Wheal Gertrude were used as count house and workshops for several of the smaller mines.

If it was not built as the count house, it must have been built after the closure of Wheal Gertrude. The mine was still active in 1826, as the adventurers were preparing to erect an engine in that year. It had by then been taken over by a London company, and it linked underground with Wheal Towan; there was an adit stretching all the way from Mingoose to Porthtowan. But it must have closed soon after this, for by 1847, when it was leased by the church, it was already a well-established house with a history as a kidley-wink. It might have been built, perhaps with the stones from an engine house around 1830. On the whole, the earlier date is more likely.

Whenever it was built, it would never have been called Mingoose Villa. A 'villa' suggests to me a late Victorian, semi-detached house, with perhaps a monkey-puzzle tree in the front garden. Or a white-walled house above the Mediterranean, with yachts in the harbour below and cocktails served on the terrace. It does not fit a traditional Cornish house of stone and slate. The name would have been given to it at the end of the nineteenth century, possibly by William Henry Richards, auctioneer and valuer, who liked it well enough to enter it twice into Kelly's Directory of 1897, about the time when The Miners' Arms by the stream became Shasta Villa. It was fashionable; it had the right touch of pretension, suggesting something rather superior to the cottages round about.

For many years after moving in, we kept thinking that we would change it. But what could we change it to? There was already a Mingoose House and a Mingoose Cottage, and there was no earlier name that we could revert to. There was Wheal Gertrude, of course, but that didn't appeal to us. As it had been the home of the vicars of Mount Hawke, we could have called it the Old Vicarage or the Old Rectory. But that seemed pretentious, too, and part of a fashion for calling everything 'old'. We quite liked the idea of calling it The Count House; the name was full of historical interest. When the accounts had been inspected, the adventurers used to sit down to the count dinner. In some mines it was served on pewter made from the mine's own tin and stamped with its own seal. We could imagine them sitting around the table in our kitchen, eating their roast beef and drinking punch poured from the count house jug, decorated with the name of the mine. After the meal, the drinking would go on far into the afternoon ... But we couldn't be sure that it was true. It might never have been a count house.

As time went by, it became more difficult to change, as Martin Yelland found when he wanted to rename their cottage Boscothwyn.

Even if it seems inappropriate at first, a name grows to a person or place (just as Pep's name stuck to her; her full name is Kathleen Elizabeth Peplow). I don't think we shall ever change now, and eventually after forty years we had a slate name-plate engraved.

We have not made many changes to the house. The roofs were the original scantle slates; these were held in place by wooden pegs hooked on to a lath, and plastered underneath, a process known as 'torching'. After more than a century, the pegs had rotted and a lot of the plaster, very dry, crumbly, gritty material containing sea-sand and cows' hair, had fallen away. The traditional way of dealing with this was to give the roof a cement wash, so that the slates were held from above rather than below. This had been done at the front of the house, where the roof is exposed to the wind from the sea.

Mingoose Villa in the nineteen-twenties

In the eighties we had a new roof of Delabole slate. The married quarters at RAF St Eval were being refurbished, the wartime slate replaced by asbestos. I bought the roof of a terrace of three houses and the slates were delivered and stacked on the front lawn. They were random slates of all different sizes and the two slaters, father and son, had to select them carefully so that they overlapped and decreased in size as they mounted to the ridge.

The kitchen floor and hallway were originally paved with quarry tiles in a pattern of black, red and cream. They must have been very bright when new, but they have mellowed over the years, where they still remain in the hall. In the kitchen where the ale-drinkers once sat they had broken and the space between filled with concrete. There were two large slate slabs, in the doorway and in front of the fireplace. This slab had been re-used when the house was built, because it was one side of a water tank, probably from a mine. There are four drill holes for the iron rods which clamped the cistern together. When the City Hall in Truro was demolished to be replaced by the Hall for Cornwall they found the original 1846 slate beneath a wooden floor. I was able to get some of the pieces to complete the slate floor in the kitchen. It took six men to carry the largest slab.

The windows were replaced by modern sashes, probably just after the war. They give the exterior a very bare, uninhabited look and I should like to restore the sixteen-pane windows that the house had in the old postcard. Inside, we have exposed a lot of stone,

Evening light at Chapel Porth

opening up two fireplaces, including the big, wide chimney in the kitchen and removing the plaster from the wall which was once the outside of the house, in the passage between the kitchen and the dairy, which we call the back kitchen. The stones here have the marks of ivy suckers still on them, like the claws of birds.

We have stripped the doors, but not the staircase; we have not painted any beams black. It would not surprise me if stripped pine and exposed stone come to seem unfashionable. I would have few regrets for the pine, having spent too many hours working away at it with sandpaper, scarsten scrapers and bits of broken glass. But I should miss the stones, the variety of colour and texture, the different shapes, the sense of closeness to the builders who first placed them in position.

The house is full of ghosts. One part of me says that it is just a collection of rooms, of spaces bounded by stone or lath and plaster; it cannot be any different from a group of rooms in a modern building. And yet I feel the presence of those who built it and who lived here before. On a winter's evening between four and five, when it is nearly dark outside and I go to draw the curtains, I pause with my hand on the material, arrested in what I am doing. I look through the window pane and see the valley in blackness, the sea still catching the light; the bare branches of the trees are silhouetted against the wild sky. At such a moment I feel that I am repeating an action performed many times before.

I wake up at night and feel a presence in the room. Pep says she sometimes sees a girl with fair hair and in a long dress, standing at the foot of the bed. Everyone finds Peter's room, the one at the back in which he was born, the most 'ghostly' in the house. No one ever feels any menace from these presences.

People disappear, leaving few traces behind. They remain as memories in the minds of others or in stories that are handed down. Mrs Oram takes summer visitors. I.J. Richards comes home from lappy-side, fumbling with the latch. The Coleman children light candles under the staircase. In the middle of the night eight-year-old Joy creeps down the stairs and into bed with red-headed Doris in the back kitchen. Mrs Johns runs a general store from the same room, which is now called the shop. Bill Morrison buys lemonade from her in a marble-stoppered bottle; there is always a crate lying on its side by the door.

The house is untenanted for a while and Bill and his cousin sleep here one night out of bravado. They think that Joe Yelland will come around playing some prank, pretending to be a ghost, so they have a bucket of water on an upstairs window-sill, ready for him. He comes at midnight and they drive him away.

Jane Webb dreams of the days when she was a girl and one of three hundred bal-maidens at work in the valley, sorting and dressing the ore. The water-wheels turn in the night, working the stamps which pound and rattle. Audrey Winn, unable to sleep in an unfamiliar bed, tries to remember the name of a schoolmaster who lives in the house. He drives a pony and trap to Redruth each day. The house is called The Plantation because of all the trees around it. She knows his name well, but still can't recall it.

A parakeet flies into a tree in the garden. It is a beautiful bird, all yellow, green and blue. It has escaped from a mine captain who has brought it back from Brazil. Young Eddie Tredinnick climbs the tree and catches it, though it bites him badly.

The fir trees disappear. William Henry Richards returns from a farm auction and stables the pony. Constable Benney cycles past in the night, his black cape blowing in the wind and his acetylene lamp flickering. An old lady collapses and dies on the slate slab in front of the kitchen stove. A half-Spanish girl is born in one of the bedrooms and her father tears the rails out of the walls to make a fire. The vicars of Mount Hawke - Edward Montague Hamilton, Henry Stone, Henry Wheeler Brenton, William Avery, Isidore Daimpré and William Henry Allin - write their sermons in the study where I write now. They are called out to visit a dying parishioner and their manservant drives them in the pony and trap up the road to the Victory Inn, through the rain and darkness.

John Julian brews his ale in the back kitchen or brewhouse, and one of his customers breaks his neck when he falls from the path into the road. The adventurers, faintest ghosts of all, having inspected the accounts and eaten the count dinner, drink long into the afternoon and the purser's wife, whose name is Gertrude, goes around the house to draw the curtains. She pauses for a moment at one of the windows, to look down the valley at the last of the light on the sea.

143

Bibliography

Maurice H Bizley, Friendly Retreat, self-published, 1955. Reprinted by St Agnes Museum trust.

T. O. Darke, The Cornish Chough, Bradford Barton, 1971

H. L. Douch, Old Cornish Inns, Bradford Barton, 1966

A. K. Hamilton Jenkin, The Cornish Miner, Allen and Unwin, 1927
    Mines and Miners of Cornwall, 2 St Agnes - Perranporth, 1962
    Cornwall and Its People, J. M. Dent & Son, 1945

Bill Morrison, Jack of All Trades, self-published, 2001

Betty Tredinnick, Eddie Tredinnick - A St Ann's Man (1889-1983) The Journal of
    the St Agnes Museum Trust no 8

R. B Treleaven, Peregrine, the Private Life of the Peregrine Falcon, Headland Publications, 1977